Samuel French Acting Ed

M000199000

Familiar

by Danai Gurira

SAMUELFRENCH.COM   SAMUELFRENCH.CO.UK

FOR PRODUCTION ENQUIRIES

UNITED STATES AND CANADA
Info@SamuelFrench.com
1-866-598-8449

UNITED KINGDOM AND EUROPE
Plays@SamuelFrench.co.uk
020-7255-4302

Each title is subject to availability from Samuel French, depending upon country of performance. Please be aware that *FAMILIAR* may not be licensed by Samuel French in your territory. Professional and amateur producers should contact the nearest Samuel French office or licensing partner to verify availability.

MUSIC USE NOTE

Licensees are solely responsible for obtaining formal written permission from copyright owners to use copyrighted music in the performance of this play and are strongly cautioned to do so. If no such permission is obtained by the licensee, then the licensee must use only original music that the licensee owns and controls. Licensees are solely responsible and liable for all music clearances and shall indemnify the copyright owners of the play(s) and their licensing agent, Samuel French, against any costs, expenses, losses and liabilities arising from the use of music by licensees. Please contact the appropriate music licensing authority in your territory for the rights to any incidental music.

IMPORTANT BILLING AND CREDIT REQUIREMENTS

If you have obtained performance rights to this title, please refer to your licensing agreement for important billing and credit requirements.

Original music by Somi Kakoma is required for performance. Please contact your licensing representative for further information.

FAMILIAR was commissioned by Yale Repertory Theatre, New Haven, Connecticut (James Bundy, Artistic Director; Victoria Nolan, Managing Director) and received its first public performance on January 30, 2015.

FAMILIAR was produced by Playwrights Horizons, Inc. in New York City and received its New York premiere on February 12, 2016. The production was directed by Rebecca Taichman, with scenic design by Clint Ramos, costume design by Susan Hilferty, lighting design by Tyler Micoleau, and sound design by Darron L. West. The production stage manager was Cole P. Bonenberger. The cast was as follows:

MARVELOUS	Tamara Tunie
DONALD	Harold Surratt
MARGARET	Melanie Nicholls-King
NYASHA	Ito Aghayere
TENDIKAYI	Roslyn Ruff
ANNE	Myra Lucretia Taylor
CHRIS	Joby Earle
BRAD	Joe Tippett

CHARACTERS

MARVELOUS (Mai Tendi) – an African woman in her mid-sixties, matriarch

DONALD (Baba Tendi) – an African man in his mid-sixties, Marvelous' husband

MARGARET (Mai Tongi) – an African woman in her fifties, Marvelous' youngest sister

NYASHA – American-Zimbabwean young woman in her late twenties, Marvelous and Donald's youngest daughter

TENDIKAYI – American-Zimbabwean woman in her mid-thirties, Marvelous and Donald's oldest daughter

ANNE (Mai Carol) – an African woman in her late sixties, Marvelous' eldest sister

CHRIS – a Caucasian American man, Tendikayi's fiancé, mid-thirties

BRAD – a Caucasian American man, Chris' cousin, mid-thirties

SETTING

Marvelous and Donald's house, an upper-middle-class suburb of Minneapolis, Minnesota

TIME

Now...why not.

ACT ONE

Scene One

(The living room of an upper-middle-class Midwestern home. The room is complete with an open dining room area, sofa, loveseat, a grand glass coffee table, wooden floors, and an expensive looking rug in the center of the room. The living room opens out into the kitchen. There is a hallway leading to a study, in which we can see [when open] books abound and a large exercise ball rests at the center of the room. Other doors lead to a bathroom, and a doorway leads upstairs. An all-American home except for one detail that gives away its non-American ownership: a large, colorful display of the map of Zimbabwe. Bright and elaborate, it is similar to what one would find in a travel agent's office.)

(DONALD CHINYARAMWIRA, *a gentle, distinguished African man in his mid-sixties, stares up at the map, standing before it. He adjusts it slightly. He steps back and stares at it as if admiring his handiwork. He holds a TV remote; a random college football game blares on the TV.* Just then his wife,* **DR. MARVELOUS CHINYARAMWIRA,** *steps out of the kitchen into the dining room – which is*

---

*A license to produce *Familiar* does not include the right to use any pre-recorded football games. Licensees should create their own original sound effects.

7

covered in baked goods. It looks something like a confectionary table. Hands gloved and carrying a tray of bread rolls, **MARVELOUS** *places the rolls on the already crowded table.* **DONALD** *moves toward her as though readying himself to speak. She glimpses over at him and checks to see what he has placed on the wall.)*

(Suddenly stopping what she is doing, wiping her hands on her apron, she goes into the living room and removes the map from the wall.)

DONALD. Listen...Marvi.

MARVELOUS. What? Ichi chirikutsvageyi muno? Hazviite!

DONALD. We need to...

MARVELOUS. I won't have it. Wazvinzwa?! [Why would you want this in here? I won't have it! Do you understand?!]

DONALD. Look, Marvelous...

MARVELOUS. Of course you don't.

> *(She takes the map to the closet and stuffs it inside.)*

I don't even have time for this. And turn down that TV.

> *(She heads back to the kitchen.)*

Nyasha! Ha! How many times Mwanawangu! Come down!

NYASHA. *(Exiting her bedroom in her pajamas, holding an African instrument.)* Morning Mom.

MARVELOUS. Good morning?! It's near noon! Come greet your mother ah!

NYASHA. *(Embracing her mother with love but not an overwhelming amount of warmth.)* How are you doing?

MARVELOUS. Good! Busy! Glad you finally made it with that snowstorm! I couldn't stay up any longer.

NYASHA. Yeah. We were sitting on the tarmac in Wisconsin for three hours! A nice welcome home from Minnesota. Not that New York is much better. Morning Dad!

DONALD. Good morning my sweetheart.

> *(They greet with great warmth and affection; he kisses her on the forehead.)*

I can't wait to hear about your trip home!

MARVELOUS. Well I'm just glad you made it back from there in one piece!

NYASHA. OH my goodness, it's so beautiful! I went to Vic Falls and Great Zimbabwe! I think I had a visitation with an ancestor there Mom! You guys should really think about going back, reconnect.

MARVELOUS. *(Glimpsing over at DONALD.)* Ah, ha, not really in the cards my dahling. Baba Tendi! You can't watch football all day kani! / Go check the mail, I think I heard the truck.

DONALD. But I just / –
(Reluctantly.) Ya...

> **(MARVELOUS** *exits into the kitchen.)*

NYASHA. Mom. Dad – check out my mbira.

> *(Showing DONALD her mbira.)*

DONALD. Oh! You brought it!

NYASHA. Of course! I got it from this amazing musician in Mbare.

DONALD. *(With yearning admiration.)* Oh wow. You went to Mbare? How was it?

NYASHA. It was...a lot! But so alive, even with all the issues you know? You read my blog right?

DONALD. Of course I did.

NYASHA. And...

DONALD. I told you it was... I was deeply indicted.

NYASHA. Yeah, you did say that.

> *(Beat.)*

You gotta break that down for me more Dad.

DONALD. Ya. Soon.

> *(Beat.)*

DONALD. Can you play some?

NYASHA. Only when the spirit is right, my teacher says.

(**MARVELOUS** *re-enters.*)

MARVELOUS. Ah! Donald!

DONALD. I'm going, I'm going...

(*He exits.*)

MARVELOUS. Help me Nyasha.

(**NYASHA** *stuffs her mbira in the study and helps her mother place baked goods around the dining room.*)

NYASHA. Did you read my blog yet?

MARVELOUS. Oh, I will! I just have had such an intense time at work my dear!

(*Beat.*)

NYASHA. So. How is work?

MARVELOUS. Great!! Our grant to research the function of DNA in determining inheritance at a molecular level came through so we are busy.

NYASHA. Great.

(*Awkward silence.*)

MARVELOUS. Now where is your aunt?

NYASHA. Auntie Maggie? Is she here? In a fabulous new weave I imagine?

MARVELOUS. Of course. Well, not that new...

NYASHA. Ouch. So where is the happy couple?

MARVELOUS. Tendi should be by soon.

NYASHA. Well, what should I do?

MARVELOUS. Plenty. And, don't forget you are performing –

NYASHA. That's at the wedding.

MARVELOUS. Yes, but, well, we thought you could do a little bit for us tonight at the rehearsal dinner –

NYASHA. MOM! You KNOW how I do not do the impromptu thing.

MARVELOUS. You have *(Looks at her watch.)* exactly seven hours till the dinner – you can do it! Tendi claims you are quite good / or you can just play your violin again, that would be amazing!

NYASHA. *Quite* good?! Wow.

MOM! My violin?! I haven't played that since you stopped forcing me to in the ninth grade! Not everyone can be a biochemist Mother!

MARVELOUS. Ah! Mwanawangu! If you don't want to help your sister / you don't have to. It's that simple –

NYASHA. Oh my God!! Really with the guilt-tripping?

> *(**PROFESSOR MARGARET MUNYEWA** enters from the washroom. She is Marvelous' youngest sister, indeed decked out – though not really well put together – with a luscious, long weave.)*

MARGARET. EH! EH! Noise! What are you two shouting about already?

NYASHA. Hi Auntie Maggie.

MARGARET. "Hi Auntie Maggie." Is that how you greet your mainini [younger aunt]? When was the last time you saw me eh?

NYASHA. It's been a while –

MARGARET. Do you know what you would be doing for me back home?

NYASHA. Yes.

MARGARET. So?

> *(**NYASHA** kneels on the floor and her aunt sits down on the chair next to her.)*

NYASHA. Makadii Mainini? [How are you Aunt?] *(Clapping her hands in the traditional Shona way.)*

MARGARET. *(Deeply amused.)* Ndiripo Makadii wo? [I am well, how are you?]

NYASHA. Ini ndiripo zvangu.

MARGARET. NOT "Ini INdiripooo" Ndiripo. [I am well.]

NYASHA. Ndiripo.

MARGARET. Exactly. Very good. You get a C+. I thought your pronunciation would be better since the trip!

> *(They embrace with love and warmth that is allowed between an aunt and a niece who do not have the baggage of a mother and a daughter.)*

NYASHA. Come on! I sounded Haitian before the trip! Are the boys coming?

MARGARET. Ah, well, they can't...they can't make it.

MARVELOUS. Okay, you two! Nyasha, you need to shower and dress. We don't have a lot of time. Oh! And we must squeeze some shopping in to get Nyasha something nice to wear / – I grabbed a couple items at Nordstroms –

NYASHA. Get Nyasha something nice to wear?

MARGARET. Just let it go Nyasha.

MARVELOUS. I would just like you to look like –

NYASHA. Like what?

MARGARET. Oh God.

MARVELOUS. Like you are going to a rehearsal dinner and a wedding and not to an open microphone performance or whatever –

NYASHA. I have no intention / to change up MY style for your sense of conformist propriety –

MARGARET. LADIES!

> (**DONALD** *comes in from outside.*)

MARVELOUS. This is what you get for raising your child in the West. "Conformist propriety"! When I was growing up we would NEVA / talk to our parents like that –

NYASHA. Here we go.

> (**MARVELOUS**' *phone beeps in her apron pocket.*)

MARVELOUS. Oh! That is me I believe!

> *(Fishing it out, she reads a text and stops dead in her tracks.)*

Oh no, oh no, oh no. Oh Jesus no. Maihwee kani! [Oh my gosh!]

MARGARET. What is it?

MARVELOUS. Maggie, Read this. Read it.

(Ignoring **NYASHA.***)*

TODAY?!! / You were supposed to HANDLE this MAGGIE!

MARGARET. I tried!

MARVELOUS. AIWA KANI! [NO MAN!] *Tried?* WHY didn't you do what I commanded?!

MARGARET. Commanded? Wow. I tried Marvi. You know her kani [man].

(Exiting toward kitchen.)

MARVELOUS. NO. Do something right for once.

(Everyone starts to exit.)

NYASHA. Whoa.

(Beat.)

What is going on?

MARGARET. Your Auntie Anne is coming.

NYASHA. Shouldn't it be a good thing that Auntie Anne is coming?

DONALD. Ahhh...

*(***DONALD** *straightens out the map on his way to the restroom.* **MARGARET** *pours herself another glass of Cabernet Sauvignon.)*

NYASHA. What is up with *that* by the way?

MARGARET. What?

NYASHA. THIS. *(Pointing at the map.)*

MARGARET. Oh God, she takes it down, he puts it up. In fact, just take it down. Just take it down.

*(***MARGARET** *gets up, laboring to get it off the wall.)*

NYASHA. The map of Zim? SO not their style!

(**MARVELOUS** *enters with a tray of lasagna.*)

NYASHA. Isn't it a little early for lunch?

MARVELOUS. Watch out Nyasha!

NYASHA. Sorry!

> (*Beat.*)

I thought we were supposed to have lunch with Tendi and Chris?

> (**MARVELOUS** *dishes lasagna out ferociously.*)

MARVELOUS. O. [Here.]

> (*Handing a plate to her husband.*)
>
> (*They all sit and watch her; she is moving like lightening, her face taut.*)

DONALD! TAKE THE PLATE!

DONALD. I thought you were serving Nyasha.

MARVELOUS. Why would I serve Nyasha first? Are you not the man of the house?

> (**MARVELOUS** *hands each of them their plates, moving with frightening precision and aggression.*)

(*To no one in particular.*) If she thinks she can just pitch up out of the BLUES and take over MY child's wedding – How did she even get money for a ticket?! Maggie?!

MARGARET. I...I haven't a clue. Honestly.

DONALD. Hmm hmm. It's really good lasagna. Very, very good. The pecans, great touch.

NYASHA. Mom? You okay?

> (**MARVELOUS** *catches herself and attempts to return to normal.*)

MARVELOUS. (*Taking a seat.*) Anyway, anyway, anyway. Thank you my dear, I am fine.

NYASHA. Uh...so...Auntie! How goes everything?

MARGARET. Yes! I have a new product out –

MARVELOUS. How is your real job? Your professorship? I mean what is the point?!

MARGARET. The point?

MARVELOUS. To flail around as an adjunct without tenure for a decade!

MARGARET. / Ah!

DONALD. / Eeeish.

NYASHA. Ah, so Dad!

DONALD. Yes?

NYASHA. Did...ahh did white boy ask you for her hand at least?

MARVELOUS. His name is Christopher kiddo, don't be such a hoodlum. And yes, Donald, talk about *that*.

MARGARET. *(Under her breath.)* Maiwee...

DONALD. Ya, okay, well, he is very pleasant.

NYASHA. I can't believe I haven't even met the guy yet.

DONALD. He is very worldly, he spent some time in South Asia and also Western Africa –

NYASHA. Where in Africa?

DONALD. Oh – I'm not sure, eh maybe Gabon or Gambia. Anyway – he asked me if he could ask for Tendikayi's hand and I said yes, if she would agree of course.

NYASHA. What does he do?

DONALD. He works with human rights and debt cancellation, things like that – it's an international nonprofit that he co-founded.

NYASHA. Huh. He probably knows more about Africa than she does. How long have they been dating?

MARGARET. About seven months, don't you and Tendi talk?

NYASHA. Apparently not enough seeing as I'm not even a bridesmaid!

MARGARET. *(Sarcasm dripping.)* She had to use her sisters of the International Church Ministries of what what –

MARVELOUS. Maggie. Do. Not. Get. Me started.

MARGARET. You can wear whatever you like Nana! I got a fantastic canary yellow dress! With matching pumps! All on sale at Neimans!

MARVELOUS. I hope that was a *great* sale.

MARGARET *(Carefully.)* It was.

>   *(Beat.)*

MARVELOUS. Anyway. When she comes by, someone should try to talk to her.

NYASHA. / Yeah maybe.

MARGARET. Oh God. The day before the wedding?!

NYASHA. Surprised you care Mom. Isn't this how you would have it? All Christianized?

MARVELOUS. There is nothing Christian about leaving your family out of your wedding party! Don't be such a heathen! It's just that happy clappy church of hers. Why she didn't stay at United Lutheran where she was raised I'll never know. I just hope they don't wave their hands in the air, randomly shouting "Halleluia." She should have let Reverend Ekelund do the service, but oh no, she has to use her happy clappy pastor. Who still reeks of his mummy's milk and dresses like a motorbiker! He's probably getting a fresh tattoo to commemorate the occasion!

NYASHA. Well did they do marriage counseling at least?

MARVELOUS. Yes, at that church.

>   *(Beat.)*

NYASHA. So THAT'S why they are rushing –

MARVELOUS. They are not rushing –

NYASHA. It's the Christian thing.

MARGARET. What Christian thing?

NYASHA. Duhh! They are trying to hold out.

MARGARET. Nyash, can you ever wait for appropriate time and place to open your mouth?

NYASHA. Why else in the world would they have a winter wedding in Minnesota!

MARVELOUS. If they are "holding out" then good for them! At least I raised one child right!

NYASHA. Wow.

MARVELOUS. Ya. You generation of today, it's like, you get with this one and do it with him, it doesn't work out, then you get with that one and do it with him, it doesn't work out, and you are just going from person to person! Before you know it your genitals are like bus stops, one leaves, another arrives!

MARGARET. *(Laughing uproariously.)* AHH HAHAHA!!

NYASHA. MOM!

> *(**DONALD** shakes his head, blushing under his dark skin.)*

MARGARET. *(Kinda impressed.)* That was pretty good Marvi!

MARVELOUS. *(Smugly.)* Because it is true, baby sister!

NYASHA. Anyway! Are we doing any African traditional stuff, respect our ancestors up in here or are you just letting this white boy get off real easy?

MARGARET. Aha!

DONALD. Hmm.

MARVELOUS. AH AH AH! We are going to be classy, civilized and *modern.*

NYASHA. Since when was all this church stuff civilized and modern?!

> *(The door is heard unlocking.)*

TENDI. Hello!

MARVELOUS. Hey? Tendi?!

TENDI. Yeah Mom, hey everyone!

> *(**TENDIKAYI** enters.)*

MARGARET. The Bride Awuya!

> *(Ululating.)*

Wholololo!

> *(**MARVELOUS** joins in and jumps up. They start to dance around **TENDI**, singing, ululating.)*

MARVELOUS. Whololololo, *(Dancing gently, all her Africanness fully on display.)* all the children are here!

> *(**MARGARET** and **DONALD** join in, **DONALD** grabbing the base of the song. **MARVELOUS**, **MARGARET**, and **DONALD** sing as they dance around **TENDI**, celebrating her arrival:)*

MARGARET, DONALD & MARVELOUS.

> MAKOROKOTO! MAKOROKOTO, MAKOROKOTO! AYA NDIWO MAKOROKOTO! AYA NDIWO MAKOROKOTO! [CONGRATULATIONS, CONGRATULATIONS!]

> *(**TENDI** dances along with them, joining in here and there where she can.)*

> *(**NYASHA** joins in also; pleased to see a rare display of her family expressing their Africanness.)*

MARGARET. Wauya! [You have come!]

MARVELOUS. How are you? LOVE the hair!

TENDI. Thanks Mom, yeah, just finished it, took FOREVER! And those Congolese ladies can puuull! / I lost nerve function in my scalp!

MARGARET. *(Laughing.)* I know!

MARVELOUS. You are going to tie it up nicely for the wedding of course!

TENDI. Of course Mother. Hey baby sis?

NYASHA. *Baby?*

TENDI. *(Embracing her.)* I changed your diapers chica! How are you?!

NYASHA. Good! Congrats!

TENDI. Thanks love! Are you in your PJs? You will be ready in time for the dinner right?

NYASHA. Of course! So, where is he?

TENDI. He can't wait to meet you, he's handling a bit of family stuff. You're gonna *love* him Nyash.

NYASHA. Mukwasha ngauye nemombe!

TENDI. / Whaa...?

MARGARET. *(Cracking up.)* Ah! This one! Anogona chishona! She knows?!

MARVELOUS. *(Laughing.)* Eye! She knows! She does!

NYASHA. *(To* **MARVELOUS.***)* No thanks to you.

> *(Beat.)*

MARGARET. Ah, Nyasha –

MARVELOUS. Ah! You didn't want to learn!

NYASHA. HOW can you say a CHILD didn't want to learn a language?

MARVELOUS. YOU didn't want to learn Shona now you want to blame me!

TENDI. Oh my God. Dad, when is the game on?

NYASHA. Why can't you JUST admit it Mother? That you CHOSE not to teach your children their native tongue!

TENDI. Are we REALLY DOING THIS right now?

MARVELOUS. AH! This girl just likes to fight, that's ALL! *(Pointedly, to* **TENDI.***) SO* my daughter, you should come sample the wonderful baked goods. *(Gesturing to the dining room.)*

TENDI. Oh beautiful Mom, the salmon croquettes?

MARVELOUS. Right here, fresh out of the oven.

TENDI. Mmmmm.

NYASHA. / I was just in Zim, and I wanted to be able to / COMMUNICATE –

MARVELOUS. Is that Rachel Maddox?

NYASHA. MaddOW.

DONALD. Ya.

MARVELOUS. In the afternoon?

DONALD. I DVR'd it last night.

MARVELOUS. What is wrong with you Baba Tendi?

DONALD. I thought you were talking –

MARVELOUS. You know I don't miss Rachel. Come sit next to your mother Tendi. Oh! And I got you something borrowed!

TENDI. Fantastic!

NYASHA. I mean didn't the boys speak ONLY Shona when you moved / here and now they ONLY speak English?

TENDI. Nyasha!

MARVELOUS. SHUSH!

TENDI. Now I just gotta get something blue from Chris's mom.

MARGARET. If you want to learn Shona so bad, why didn't you stay there longer and really LEARN it?!

MARVELOUS. Mai Tongi! Don't indulge her! Look – it's Rachel –

NYASHA. I just want to know WHY you chose to discontinue a beautiful tradition. I mean Auntie *Florie* was in the liberation struggle / for God's sake –

MARVELOUS. Who told you that?

NYASHA. Auntie Ann. She also said that you guys used to –

MARVELOUS. *WHAT?!* DON'T BELIEVE ANYTHING THAT COMES OUT OF THAT WOMAN'S MOUTH NOW SHUSH!

NYASHA. Auntie, just tell me, why didn't you keep up the boys' Shona?

MARGARET. *(Beat.)* They were already put behind in school because they couldn't speak a word of English.

MARVELOUS. Anyway, anyway, anyway. Have the flowers arrived my dear?

MARGARET. Even their own cousins, you and Tendi would make fun of them.

TENDI. We did make fun – / Yeah, they are gorg Mom. Perfect. Check them out.

> *(Shows her a picture on her phone.)*

MARGARET. THANK YOU TENDI!

> (**MARGARET** *takes several large swigs from her wine glass.*)

NYASHA. / So.

MARVELOUS. / Wonderful. No red?

TENDI. No Mother.

MARGARET. / I wanted my children to have the best education, SO I only spoke to them in English.

NYASHA. Thank you Auntie. That makes sense.

(Beat.)

Mother?

MARVELOUS. EH! Child! YOU DIDN'T WANT TO LEARN! Handle her Baba Tendi, for ONCE!

(She exits. Silence a moment.)

TENDI. Why don't you just let it go. She isn't changing. Why do you do this to yourself?

NYASHA. BECAUSE! I want her to admit!

TENDI. WHAT? That no matter how many knitting circles she sat in with a bunch of white middle Americans, there was no way she was going to get rid of that thick African accent, but maybe, she could belong through having children who didn't have one?

NYASHA. But I felt like a FREAK in Zimbabwe. I look Zimbabwean, I have a Zimbabwean name, but I was ashamed to open my mouth!

DONALD. We didn't know.

NYASHA. What Dad?

DONALD. We didn't know it was possible to have you guys speak Shona like us and sound American like them.

NYASHA. So you admit it was you guys not us?

DONALD. Of course the child doesn't decide on those things –

MARGARET. *(Re-entering with another large glass of Cab.)* I can't wait until you have children and they want all sorts of answers from you! *(Laughing.)* Ohhh! I cannot wait!

> (**MARVELOUS** *re-enters with a large tray of salmon croquettes.*)

MARVELOUS. They're ready!

> *(She serves everyone ceremoniously, conspicuously skipping* **NYASHA**.*)*

MARVELOUS. Did you keep that strapless contraption?

TENDI. You mean my Vera Wang gown? Yes Mother, I kept it.

MARVELOUS. Oh, well. At least it's a crisp white. Some people are getting married in red these days. Just barbarians. But, oh gosh. I mean even just a one-shoulder would be better.

TENDI. I love my dress Mother.

MARVELOUS. Wonderful! She loves her dress!

> *(Beat.)*

TENDI. *(Getting up.)* SO, I have *SO* much to do.

> *(**DONALD** reaches for his daughter and squeezes her hand, pulling her down for a kiss on the cheek.)*

MARGARET. Anything we can help with?

TENDI. No! Thank you! I have a fantastic team in place.

MARGARET. Of course.

TENDI. Let's just be ready in time to make it to the dinner. Also, I have a little surprise for you guys.

> *(To **NYASHA**.)* And we need to have a good, ah, catch-up before you leave.

NYASHA. Yikes. Ooookay...

TENDI. How was your trip?

NYASHA. YOU didn't check out the blog either did you.

TENDI. I will, I promise!

NYASHA. Then you wonder why our country doesn't advance. Folks who are the most empowered, not even vaguely / interested.

> *(**MARVELOUS**' phone rings.)*

MARVELOUS. SHUSH! *(Looking at phone.)* These are our new in-laws. *(On the phone.)* Hellow, this is Marvelous. Hi Jennifer! It's Marvelous, yes! Yes! The whole clan is here! My youngest sister IS here! The geology professor. Flor– Florie is the one who passed, yes, she was number three. You are so sweet to remember!

Hmmm? I have plenty of platters. Thanks so much for checking!! Okay, toodles! *(She hangs up.)*

TENDI. I'm glad you guys get along.

MARVELOUS. Oh yes, she is a dear.

> *(**MARGARET** returns from refilling her glass of Cab.)*

NYASHA. SO what is the surprise Tendi?

MARVELOUS. Clues at least?

MARGARET. *(On the tipsy side of the scale.)* Hmm. Looks like we might have a small surprise for you too!

TENDI. What?

> *(**MARGARET** chuckles in the background as she sips her wine.)*

MARVELOUS. Ah! What are you laughing about Mai Tongi?

MARGARET. Ah! Nothing ka!

MARVELOUS. And you must stop drinking all that wine like there is no tomorrow coming! I don't need you –

MARGARET. You don't need me what?

> *(**MARVELOUS** does not answer.)*

You don't need me what? This is my *first* glass Mai Tendi.

MARVELOUS. It's not your first.

MARGARET. Yes it is! / How is it not my first?

DONALD. OH NO!!

NYASHA. *(They all rush to the TV.)* What the –

MARVELOUS. Baba Tendi what is wrong with you?

TENDI. Dad!

DONALD. WHAT?

MARVELOUS. We've been waiting for this game all day!!

DONALD. Ah, I'm sorry, I was –

TENDI. How's PENN STATE'S quarterback doing?

> *(**NYASHA** goes to the other side of the room; she starts going through a sun salutation.)*

DONALD. He's still out injured, this other kid, the back-up is the quarterback today –

MARGARET. That scrawny black kid?

DONALD. Ya. He's struggling man –

MARGARET. Oh, finish. They should just play him! He can rest after the season!

DONALD. They won't get through the season if he gets worse!

TENDI. / How is he supposed to *get* them through with a busted leg Auntie Maggie!

MARVELOUS. You people! SHUSH! I am trying to hear the commentators. I have to catch up, since *someone* didn't bother to let us know this was on!

DONALD. I mean, you can see what is going on – the scoreboard is right / –

MARGARET. SHHH!!

DONALD. There –

MARVELOUS. It is NOT the same Baba Tendi and you know it!

NYASHA. *(Really only to herself.)* You know the true GLOBAL sport *is* soccer! Zim has a great team, you should – / Okaaaay, MOM. / Where are the towels? Marvelous, Margaret / shush!

MARVELOUS. / SHUSH! What?

NYASHA. / I said –

MARVELOUS. / You know where the towels are kiddo!

NYASHA. Okaaaay. And on that note…

> *(**NYASHA** gathers herself, pops one more salmon croquette into her mouth, and starts toward the stairs.)*

DONALD. *(The most animated we have seen him.)* / Come on!

TENDI. *(The most animated we have seen her.)* / Catch it baby, catch it!

MARGARET. Do it… DO IT!

(NYASHA runs into the bathroom, overcome with the urge to pee.)

MARVELOUS. YES!!

DONALD. ALRIGHT, ALRIGHT!

TENDI. That's what I'm talking about baby!

MARGARET. THAT'S IT!

TENDI. *(Clapping her hands.)* Now come on, brotherman, come on –

MARVELOUS. Ya, you got the ball now DO SOMETHING WITH IT bro!

DONALD. Give him a chance –

MARVELOUS. How am I not giving him a chance Baba Tendi?

DONALD. Ah...

MARVELOUS. You are the one who said he was –

MARGARET. Ahhh! You people! I want to watch the game kani!

MARVELOUS. So watch ka!

DONALD. Nice!

(We hear the toilet flush.)

TENDI. Now run baby run!

(NYASHA comes out of the bathroom, goes to the hallway closet, and the map falls with a thud at her feet.)

MARVELOUS. *(Screeching.)* COME ON! COME ON!

TENDI. *(On her feet.)* DO IT! DO IT!!

MARGARET. *(On her feet.)* YES! YES! RUN!!

NYASHA. *(Holding the map up.)* By the way, WHAT THE FUCK with this map?!

MARVELOUS. EH EH!! LANGUAGE!!

DONALD, MARGARET & TENDI. TOUCHDOWN!!

(The doorbell rings.)

MARVELOUS. WHO is that?

TENDI. Ah! That might be my surprise!

MARVELOUS. Ah ah?

> (*A fervent knock.* **MARVELOUS** *goes to the door, staring through the peephole.*)

MAIWEE! No. No no no.

TENDI. Mom?

> (**MARVELOUS** *opens the door. Enter* **ANNE MWARIMBA**, *Marvelous' oldest sister. She carries a handbag and a large tote bag [those red, white, and blue ones that are made of some sort of woven plastic].*)

ANNE. YES KANI!!

> (*Hugging her sister with absolute abandon.*)

MARVELOUS. Hellow Annie.

ANNE. Muri right? [Are you "right" well?]

MARVELOUS. (*With a lot less enthusiasm.*) I am fine. Makadii? [How are you?]

ANNE. Ndiripo! [I am well!]

DONALD. Mai Carol! Ah!

> (*Hugging her.*)

Ndeipi? [What's going on?]

ANNE. (*Laughing.*) Ahh! Hapana! Makadii Baba Tendi? [Nothing! How are you Baba Tendi?]

DONALD. Ndiripo! [I am well!]

NYASHA. Hey Auntie Annie! HOW COOL! I just saw you in Zim!!

ANNE. (*Embracing everyone.*) Eye! Manje ndazvika! [Now I am here!] Maggie!!

TENDI. (*Deeply pleased with herself.*) This is my surprise!!

MARGARET. Oh goodness.

TENDI. (*Hugging her aunt.*) Did you get in okay?

> (**ANNE** *has stopped and is holding* **TENDI** *at arm's length, staring at her deeply. Quite emotional.*)

ANNE. Oh maiwee, maiwee, maiwee... [My God, my God, my God...] so beautiful! So...

>*(Verging on tears.)*

>*(Suddenly buoyant again.)*

Saka mwana wedu arikuchata. [So our child is getting married.] Whololololo!

>*(Ululating, she starts to sing and dance around* **TENDI** *like we saw Marvelous, Donald, and Margaret do earlier.)*

Makorokoto –

MARVELOUS. SHHHHH! Yes, she is getting married – but –

ANNE. Saka toita rooraka. [So we do the brideprice ceremony.]

MARVELOUS. AH AH! Sisi, you are here and that is – what – it is – and we can celebrate. BUT we are not still discussing that! It is a NON-STARTER!

DONALD. Okay, okay, let's just calm down now, perhaps take a seat –

ANNE. What is the problem?

TENDI. / What's happening now?

MARVELOUS. / You know what! I knew it! I knew it!! WHY are you coming here to do this imi! / You ALWAYS –

ANNE. / What? IT must be done iwe! / *I always what?*

MARVELOUS. / NO! It must not! We are NOT in Zimbabwe!

NYASHA. / What is going on right now?

ANNE. Saka?! [So?!] Do you know what can happen to a marriage if roora is not done properly?

MARVELOUS. Heyi! Imi makupenga shuwa! [You are crazy!] Was it done for you?

ANNE. Of course!

MARVELOUS. And look what became of *that* marriage!

DONALD. Eieesh!

ANNE. Iwe! [You!] He hehe, Iwe! You think you are a white now eh? Just because makugara [you are living] in this white man's land eh! / Now you want to judge me?! I am here to bless OUR child!

MARVELOUS. As IF you wouldn't live here if you could! You think this is blessing? This is a cursing imi! Where is this in the bible eh? / OUR CHILD?! What blessing is this!

ANNE. IWE!! The ways WE do things were there BEFORE we got the bible! /

MARVELOUS. You are such a liar! All these years going to church pretending to be a Christian!

ANNE. Pretending yeyi [how]? We can do our customs AND be Christians!

MARVELOUS. NO! NOT THIS ONE!!

ANNE. Baba Tendi, Baba Tendi? What is her problem shuwa [surely]?

MARVELOUS. Don't you dare come in my house and try to turn my husband against me in my very face!

MARGARET. Marvi!

DONALD. Oh my God.

ANNE. Eeey! Fine! We can let Tendi decide for herself.

MARGARET. Exactly.

MARVELOUS. NO! She, is *my* child and I say NO!

MARGARET. Okay.

MARVELOUS. / You are going to DRIVE this mukwasha away!

ANNE. OUR CHILD! / Why would I want to drive him away? / If he can't get embrace this then he is not the one picked for her –

MARVELOUS. Because *your* children neva even – / Picked for her by who? By who?! By you?

ANNE. Never what? Never what? By our ancestors!

MARVELOUS. OH MY GOD! Our Ancestors ARE DEAD!!

ANNE. But they don't want our customs to die also!

MARVELOUS. You listen to me! This is MY child! I raised her! I fed her, clothed her –

ANNE. YOU! You think that means she is not our child also? We are ALL her mothers! And I, ini AmaiGURU [Oldest Aunt] am saying these customs cannot die.

> (**TENDI***'s fiancé,* **CHRIS,** *has by now entered the house and stands near the door.* **TENDI** *silently goes to greet him and usher him in.*)

DONALD. *(Noticing the new arrival.)* Eh... Mai Tendi...

MARVELOUS. You want this little white boy from MINNETONKA to bring us some COWS?!!

DONALD. MAI TENDI!

MARVELOUS. CHII?!! [WHAT?!!]

TENDI. Mom!

> (**MARVELOUS** *and* **ANNE** *are stopped short. They look up to see the man in question standing at the door.*)

MARVELOUS. *(Instantly transforms in tone and countenance in the way only a natural pro can.)* Ohhh! Chris! How are you? I didn't know you were coming by this early!

> (*They embrace.*)

TENDI. He picked up Auntie from the airport. Chris, this is my Auntie Maggie.

CHRIS. Nice to finally meet you. I'm the little white boy from Minnetonka.

MARVELOUS. *(Forcing a far too enthusiastic laugh.)* Ha! Ahh! You are so funny Chris! Of course we can all see you are not little!

CHRIS. *(To* **MARGARET.***)* Ini ndafara kukuziva! [I am happy to meet you!]

ANNE. *(Almost charmed.)* Hey! That is quite good, but I TOLD you, it is ndafara kuku zivai. If you don't say ziva*i* then you are addressing her without the due respect! Like how you would address an equal or a kid even!

CHRIS. *Dang it!* Right, *(Blushing.)* I'm sorry, indafara kuziwa*i*.

ANNE. *(Assessing him.)* Hmmm, quite good. Mai Tongi!

MARGARET. Ndafara kuziva Chris. Welcome.

MARVELOUS. *(Giggling nervously.)* He heheheehe! Let's all go and have a seat shall we? *(Babbling.)* I'll put some tea on, oh, Chris, of course coffee for you! I have some scrumptious lasagna, pecan-crusted, you came at a good –

(She starts to rush toward the kitchen.)

TENDI. *(Stopping her.)* Mom. Please, stop.

MARVELOUS. Wha...what?

TENDI. Listen, Mom, I guess I miscalculated your reaction to all this, but it doesn't change the facts: Chris and I discussed it with Auntie and – we want to go ahead with the roora ceremony.

NYASHA. That's freaking Awesome!

MARVELOUS. *(All decorum instantly lost.)* DISCUSSED IT WITH *AUNTIE*?!

(To her elder sister.) YOU! You were telling Nyasha some nonsense too! YOU want to turn my own children against me?

ANNE. Ah!

MARVELOUS. What did she tell you?

TENDI. We just talked and she said it was a good idea / if we –

MARVELOUS. A GOOD IDEA! You *talked*? Behind my back!! All my life you have done this! Just because unejelous chete [you are jealous]!

ANNE. Jealous yeyi? Jealous yeyi? [Jealous of what?]

MARVELOUS. Handizive! [I don't know!] Because I was the one who went to the states and completed my schooling and got a good husband and you just –

MARGARET. IMI! MARVI! Nyararai! [YOU! MARVI! Be quiet!] COME ON!

ANNE. I just what? I Just WHAT?!

MARVELOUS. Don't –!

ANNE. No! Say it! WHAT IS IT?!

MARVELOUS. Getting pregnant and losing that scholarship!

DONALD. Maiwee...

NYASHA. Oh wow.

MARGARET. MARVI! Haunyari? [Have you no shame?]

MARVELOUS. Just because I stuck to my studies and kept my legs CLOSED!

MARGARET. / MARVELOUS!!

NYASHA. Geez, MOM!

ANNE. *(Advancing toward her sister.)* Iwe ka! Iwe ka!

MARVELOUS. Just because Baba appointed me as the executress of his estate and not you, even though you were *in* Zim!

ANNE. / IWE KA! [YOU!] NDICHAKUROVA! [I WILL BEAT YOU!]

DONALD. *(Jumping between the two women.)* Okay, OKAY!

MARVELOUS. Let her come Baba Tendi, let her come! She couldn't beat me up even if Arnold Schwarzenegger was here to help her! I do Jane Fonda! I can beat you with my little pinky finger!

(Holding it up as evidence.)

TENDI. MOM! STOP THIS! This was MY decision!

MARVELOUS. She TELLS you "it *must* be done"! She probably Guilted you into buying her that ticket!

TENDI. *(Regulating.)* MOM! I am doing the roora ceremony whether or not you like it. I hope you will be a part of it, but if not I am sorry about that. We came to prepare this with her and to do it before the rehearsal dinner, I *thought* you would be happy to see her! Please, just, accept so we can move forward.

*(**MARVELOUS** has stopped cold and stares at her daughter, finally on the verge of cracking, her face trembling.)*

MARVELOUS. Oh? Okay, okay, okay, fine. You see how she is Baba Tendi? Stubborn. Just like you. You think you know what you are doing, you have NO IDEA.

(Trembling, fighting for composure.) I'm sorry about all this Christopher, I have tried very hard to keep things pleasant for you.

CHRIS. Marvelous. Please. We would really like you to be a part of this.

MARVELOUS. I cannot. I do apologize, but I...I cannot.

> *(She turns and goes upstairs to her bedroom and shuts the door behind her.)*

NYASHA. Oh. My God.

MARGARET. Maiwee.

> *(She rubs **TENDI**'s back comfortingly, looking at **TENDI**'s engagement ring.)*

AH...an Olivine Peridot! Very tasteful choice. Good ratio of Magnesium to Iron. It won't tarnish on you. Very nice.

TENDI. Yeah, thanks, it's my birthstone. We didn't want to do a diamond, with how they are traded, you can't really tell what you're –

> *(Beat.)*

Oh my God Auntie

MARGARET. I know, I know.

> *(She hugs her niece.)*

TENDI. She is so...

MARGARET. I know.

> *(Beat.)*

NYASHA. So *we* haven't met – no one bothered to –

TENDI. SORRY! Nyasha Chris – Chris – Nyasha.

NYASHA. *(To **TENDI**.)* Thank you.

> *(To **CHRIS**.)* Hi. And don't worry about my mom. She'll get over it. Or not! This. Is. Going to be. Awesome.

CHRIS. Nyasha.

> *(Hugging her.)*

I've heard so much about you!

NYASHA. Some good I hope! *(Giving her sister a long look.)*

CHRIS. Ah…

NYASHA. Auntie, can I take your stuff?

ANNE. Eye, Maita mwanawangu. [Yes, thank you my child.]

    (**NYASHA** *exits upstairs with Anne's bags.*)

NYASHA. *(Really excited.)* You can sleep in my room!

DONALD. You arrived well?

ANNE. Ten-hour layover in Amsterdam. Imi.

DONALD. Yeah, sorry about that, but I'm glad you're here. Garai, garai. [Sit down, sit down.]

MARGARET. Kwakadei kumba? [How are things at home?]

ANNE. Ah…things are, hey, they are hard ka! What do you think?

DONALD. Saka…

TENDI. / Auntie, we don't want to rush you, and I am so sorry about my mom but we would love to get this started as soon as –

ANNE. Ah! Mwanawangu! [My child!] Don't you know not to rush your elders!

TENDI. I'm sorry Auntie, it's just we are on a bit of a time crunch and –

ANNE. Ah! Baba Tendi! Zvakawoma! [It's a shame!]

DONALD. Shuwa. Shuwa.

ANNE. Fine. Let me go wash. Show me where to go ka! And get a wooden bowl and a blanket.

DONALD. Anything else you need.

TENDI. A what?

DONALD. Do you want anything to eat, to drink?

ANNE. After. Let me wash.

TENDI. Oh, man. Okay, ahh – this way. *(Leading her upstairs.)* You won't be too long right?

ANNE. Ah! How can you ask me that? What did I say? Don't rush you're elders! I'm coming from AFRICA! A FAR way! I have to wash ka! Tsika mwanawangu Ah! [Manners my child!]

TENDI. Of course, of course. Sorry Auntie. This way Auntie –

> (**TENDI** *leads* **ANNE** *upstairs,* **MARGARET** *follows behind.*)
>
> (**DONALD** *and* **CHRIS** *are left standing in the living room, awkwardly, neither quite knowing what to do next.*)
>
> (*Finally:*)

CHRIS. Man. That lasagna does look good.

DONALD. Oh yes, have some! Have some!

> (*He rushes to give him a plate.*)

Have a seat!

CHRIS. Thanks! (*Eating some.*)

DONALD. And, ah, sorry about the...eh...display...

CHRIS. Oh God, Donald, nothing to apologize for! I get it. Family. Everyone has one. Mmmm... Scrumptious.

DONALD. Hmm hmm...

TENDI. (*Coming downstairs. Looking at the watch on her phone.*) Oh man, oh man.

DONALD. Come here. Take a seat. It will be fine.

TENDI. Oh God Dad.

DONALD. It will be fine my darling.

TENDI. You promise?

DONALD. (*Laughing.*) Yes! I also promise you I am going to eviscerate you in that chess game.

TENDI. Oh, come on Dad! You know you're toast with that game!

DONALD. No! I have still got one move left!

TENDI. Your queen is gone, I have all your pawns –

DONALD. NOT all!

TENDI. Okay you have like one left –

DONALD. And he suffices!

TENDI. Okay! Okay. I would Love to see how you get yourself out of check. I cannot wait!

DONALD. You play her yet Chris?

CHRIS. Well / I'm trying to...

TENDI. No, he can't play –

DONALD. AH! You better learn! So! You guys excited?

CHRIS. Gosh yes.

TENDI. Yes. It's –

> *(Looking deeply into her fiancé's eyes.)*

It's so time...

CHRIS. Yeah...

TENDI. I've got to go round up these African women!

DONALD. Good luck on that one!

TENDI. Yeah...

> *(She gets up to the bedrooms. **ANNE** enters from the landing with bathrobe and shower cap.)*

ANNE. Eh, Tendi, come here.

TENDI. Auntie, we need to move, I have a lot on my pl–

ANNE. Listen! Get the wooden bowl, and some blankets, and do you have a mutsvairo?

TENDI. A what?

ANNE. Ah! They taught you *no* Shona hey? Maiwee. A broom! An African broom.

> *(She mimics what sweeping with this broom would look like.)*

TENDI. I have no idea.

ANNE. Find one. And if not, make one!

TENDI. Auntie, you can't be serious.

ANNE. *(Starting to head back to the bathroom.)* I am *very* serious! And we need a munyai!

TENDI. A *what*?

ANNE. Where is the gotwe [youngest]? CAROL! I mean, what is her name, NYASHA! And feed your husband.

TENDI. He is eating!

ANNE. Ah ah ah! He is too thin! People will talk!

TENDI. *(Following her.)* / What people? Auntie!

CHRIS. Oh, that's just my metabolism Auntie – *(Trailing off.)* She feeds me...

DONALD. Oh boy.

    (Beat.)

Not sure if you guys realize what you signed up for.

CHRIS. I'm starting to get that.

    (Beat.)

Anyway! I hope you can teach me some chess moves!

DONALD. I thought that was how you wooed her!

CHRIS. No! It was almost my undoing! One of her non-negotiables! College-educated, check. Clean record, check. Christian, check. Chess master – no? Oh we have a problem! You're a tough example to follow!

DONALD. Don't worry, I'll give you some tips.

CHRIS. Thanks, I appreciate that...Dad.

    (Beat.)

DONALD. So why did you decide to do, eh, roora, the brideprice?

CHRIS. Well, we wanted to be respectful first of all –

DONALD. Respectful to who?

CHRIS. Well, Tendi and I felt –

DONALD. What?

CHRIS. Honestly, we wanted to respect your culture. I mean, it felt like it was important to preserve a tradition. I mean, it just feels right to honor something ancient, something that is in your, ah, your heritage.

    (Beat.)

DONALD. Well, that's good. It is. Just – know this. Concerning Auntie Anne, you are dealing with a real Mashona woman. So...just...be strong my man. Be strong. You should get through it okay. I hope.

CHRIS. What exactly –

    (Enter NYASHA, still in her pajamas.)

NYASHA. Oh my God.

(She scurries around looking in cupboards high and low.)

DONALD. What?

NYASHA. I have to find a bucket.

DONALD. For what?

NYASHA. For Auntie. Anne. Auntie Anne wants a bucket.

DONALD. For –

NYASHA. She calls me into the bathroom, she's like stark buck naked, covered in soap from head to toe and she's *in* the shower but she wants a bucket. I tell her she is not in Africa, she can just run the shower but she says she likes to wash with a bucket! When I tried to argue with her she stepped out of the shower yelling at me in Shona – shaking her –

DONALD. OKAY okay okay, it's in that closet. My God.

NYASHA. I am So traumatized. *(Finds bucket and exits.)*

DONALD. Good God.

CHRIS. Wow.

> *(Beat.)*

DONALD. *(Looking around.)* And we better get this place cleaned up before Marvelous comes out of self-imposed exile. *(Starts to gather up some cups.)*

CHRIS. How do you do it?

DONALD. Do what?

CHRIS. Stay so loyal, so in tune with your spouse, for so long in your case?

DONALD. Ha...you listen, you compromise, you persevere. And, it would behoove me to add, you also never really have a fucking clue, currently, I certainly don't.

> *(Beat.)*

We've...we've been...we've been...

CHRIS. What?

DONALD. We've been in a bit of...a bit of an odd gear.

CHRIS. You and Marvelous?

DONALD. Ya. Where...where, not a lot gets said. Nothing actually. The thing you need to say, you seem to never say.

CHRIS. Okay.

DONALD. Ya.

CHRIS. Communication.

DONALD. Ya. That thing.

CHRIS. Do you want to talk more about it?

DONALD. No.

CHRIS. Okay. Well Tendi and I have been doing a lot of premarital counseling – one of the things they keep pummeling into us is the idea of having an awareness of the effect of our actions, or inactions on your partner, how silence, or actions that aren't discussed first or shared can break trust, sometimes irrevocably and you can –

DONALD. *(Cutting him off.)* Do you play squash? Have some of this.

> *(He pulls out a bottle of whiskey from a cupboard and pours it into CHRIS' cup.)*

CHRIS. Huh? Ahh...okay, it's just a little early for me –

DONALD. Oh come on! Drink up man! *Do* you play squash?

CHRIS. Ahh, no –

DONALD. Well, that's another thing you are gonna learn!

> *(DONALD pours himself some whiskey and throws it back. He pours more in his teacup.)*

CHRIS. Okaaaay... *(Drinking.)* Ahhhh...

DONALD. There you go.

CHRIS. Ya. Woah.

> *(Beat.)*

Our, um our counselor says role-play, ah, practice can really help say things that you may find hard to say. So. Do you want to tell me what you can't tell her maybe? Practice?

DONALD. No.

CHRIS. Okay. That's fine, that's fine.

    (Beat.)

You wanna pray about it?

    (Beat.)

DONALD. No.

CHRIS. No problem. Noooo problem at all.

    (A couple awkward beats.)

So where is everyone?

DONALD. Let's just wait here till the storm settles. You learn when to just lay low. Let's hope she doesn't come out here and bake. That's her thing.

    (Beat.)

ANNE. *(Coming out of a bedroom in her dress slip and African headwrap.)* Maggie! Unzai [bring] an IRON! *(Seeing the gentlemen.)* Ah! *(She scurries back.)*

DONALD. Grab that bottle, let's get out of here!

    (They quickly dart out of the living room and into Marvelous' study.)

    (**TENDI** *re-enters into living room area, texting rabidly.* **NYASHA** *rushes in, still pajama-clad.)*

TENDI. *(To no one in particular.)* COME ON PEOPLE!

NYASHA. Your crazy Aunt Maggie was trying to get me to buy her latest direct sales bullshit! She is fucking nuts!

TENDI. I know you are an artist and free-spirited and all, but can you refrain from all the cussing?

NYASHA. Okay, careful how I talk in front of the Holier than thou one.

TENDI. That's not fair. I never imposed my beliefs on you.

NYASHA. True dat. True dat.

    (Beat.)

TENDI. Thank you. What is she selling this time?

NYASHA. Fake coffee or some such!

TENDI. Oh God. What is *wrong* with her?

NYASHA. I know, and she has a PhD! Mom's right. *(Imitating her mother.)* "What's the point if you turn into a peddler!"

TENDI. What do you think of Chris?

NYASHA. He seems great. Love the work he's doing.

TENDI. I knew you would!

NYASHA. And I love that you're doing roora by the way.

TENDI. Yeah?

NYASHA. We are AFRICANS man! In Zim there is NO marriage without it. It IS the marriage.

TENDI. Huh. Well then! It was something we wanted to try to do. But man! Where are they?!

(She crosses to the hallway, bellowing:)

AUNTIE ANNE!

NYASHA. Please. In Zim, while I was there, I heard a story about a family that waited five hours for roora to start. Just sitting outside the gate!

TENDI. OH MY GOD!! That is not – that Cannot happen here. She needs to – Alright, alright, alright. *(Calming herself, goes back to texting and checking her phone rabidly.)*

Ah so...Nyasha! Let's have our catch-up.

NYASHA. Oh, yeah, let's.

(Beat.)

/ So –

TENDI. How goes...ah...work.

NYASHA. It's great. I have picked up a lot of new feng shui clients. It's really building.

TENDI. And the music?

NYASHA. Awesome. Going home was so amazing for it, I really think I found my voice. You'll see, I wrote a song for the wedding.

TENDI. Thanks hon, I can't wait to hear it.

(Beat.)

So / I'm just gonna ask Nyash –

NYASHA. So, yeah / I wanted to talk to you about –

TENDI. What is *your* plan?

NYASHA. My plan?

TENDI. Yes. Your goals, five-year, ten-year, / where do you want to be and what are you doing to get there?

NYASHA. Tendi!

TENDI. I mean, you have to ask yourself. When do I give up.

NYASHA. Excuse me?

TENDI. Hear me out. When do I let go of this dream that might have been a little beyond my reach, something that I constructed but that God did not design me / for and move on to that other thing.

NYASHA. God? OH God. WHAT other thing?

TENDI. The thing that will pay your bills / and give you a fulfilled life.

NYASHA. Pay my –?!! I am doing AMAZING stuff if you actually EVER took the time to pay any attention.

TENDI. Listen, you can't keep getting Daddy loans.

NYASHA. Oh my God. For real? He told you?

TENDI. Mom and Dad came here from Zim when they were barely adults and built this great life and we have to build more to make them proud, not set them back.

NYASHA. ENOUGH. Just because you sold out and became a conventional *lawyer* doesn't mean –

TENDI. / Conventional! That *convention* is what Dad does! It paid for the clothes on your back!

NYASHA. That I have to kill my joy to make you happy. Dad is a grown man. If he doesn't want to give me a loan –

TENDI. You are his BABY GIRL! You think he can bear the thought of you not being able to pay your bills?!

NYASHA. It was for my trip to Zim *actually* and it was ONE TIME.

TENDI. It was a lot of money.

NYASHA. Oh my God.

TENDI. Look, I am not trying to humiliate you. / But I Know that this was not the first time. I know that Dad has a direct deposit monthly into your account and I want you to ask him to stop it.

NYASHA. Huh!

> *(Beat.)*

This is none of your business. / He supports my art! Do you know what effing art is?

> **(MARGARET** *comes downstairs.)*

TENDI. Dad's position is changing, he isn't going to be an endless flow of dough anymore. And I love you and I will not watch you get enabled to a lifetime of dependency.

> *(Beat.)*

NYASHA. You are such a bitch.

MARGARET. Ah!

TENDI. Wow. Really.

NYASHA. A Good Christian Bitch.

MARGARET. Ah ah!

TENDI. Okay.

NYASHA. You just think you can stroll in here and shit all over my life choices? FUCK YOU TENDI. Fuck you. Fuck you with your unflappable, Jesus freak, cold as ice in Alaska bullshit. Fuck you.

TENDI. Wow. Okay.

NYASHA. You think you're so fucking perfect! You don't even include your own family in your BRIDAL party! What sort of a freaking Christian ARE *YOU*?!!

MARGARET. Nyasha!

TENDI. Really?!

NYASHA. Yeah. REALLY. Take that in your creepy cross-examining wretched heartless soul and fucking smoke it.

TENDI. This conversation has ended.

(**NYASHA** *gets up to leave.*)

NYASHA. SMOKE IT!

(*She rushes out of the front door, barefoot, in her pajamas.*)

TENDI. Well that went well.

(*Beat.* **MARGARET** *enters.*)

MARGARET. Did she just run outside in her pajamas?

TENDI. Did you hear how she spoke to me?!

MARGARET. What was going on?

TENDI. Wow. The mouth on that little monster.

MARGARET. (*Starting to laugh.*) Yeah, she did just strip you naked!

TENDI. Wanna scrub it with soap!

MARGARET. She got quite poetic with it, "creepy, cross-examining, wretched" what?!

TENDI. Please. Let's try to forget.

MARGARET. (*Still laughing.*) "...Cold as Alaska, Jesus freak." What?!

TENDI. Anyway, anyway, anyway! *You* get why I ended up choosing my bridesmaids based on my *spiritual* sisters? Mom and Nyash are taking it so personally!

MARGARET. It's your wedding, so...ya. I mean it's fine.

TENDI. Thank you.

MARGARET. Any African stuff at the ceremony though? Any Shona songs or something?

TENDI. Huh? No, just Nyash singing at the reception. I guess.

MARGARET. Oh. Okay.

(*Beat.*)

What is going on with your dad? You said something about no more cash flow something something –

TENDI. Oh. He is thinking about retiring.

MARGARET. WHAT?!

TENDI. Yeah, and you CANNOT tell anyone. Mom doesn't even know.

MARGARET. And what happens to the practice? It stops being Krasner Krasner and Chinyaramwira and just goes to being Krasner and Krasner?

TENDI. No. I become the Chinyaramwira.

(Beat.)

MARGARET. Aren't you a little young?

TENDI. There are little white boys running their daddies' firms who are much younger and less accomplished than I am.

MARGARET. Okay. Wow. Your dad retiring.

TENDI. Well...he is not really retiring. How are you doing? The boys?

MARGARET. Oh God. Please. Just pray.

TENDI. Okay. At some point you have to cut them loose Auntie.

MARGARET. I know. I know. And thanks for the...help. I'll get it back to you, I promise.

TENDI. Auntie. I said it was a gift. A *one-time* gift. But please, promise me, no more payday loans. Those guys are sharks man!

MARGARET. Yes, yes, I know. Never again.

TENDI. I hope you are reading the books and CDs I sent you.

MARGARET. Ah –

TENDI. JUST read the Suze Orman and the *Boundaries*. Just those two. *Please!*

MARGARET. Yes, yes, I will, I will, I promise. Have you made up with your mother?

TENDI. For what? She is the one who acted nuts.

MARGARET. You do handle her quite – efficiently.

TENDI. Don't cater to the drama. Her power is truly an illusion.

MARGARET. I need to learn to believe that!

TENDI. I learnt, the hard way. Try getting accused of being pregnant at twelve simply because you were the only girl in chess club.

MARGARET. Oh God. She was so hard on you.

TENDI. You think?

MARGARET. Firstborn, can't be allowed to fail I guess.

TENDI. Imagine if *I* tried to go be a singer/feng shui artist! Huh!

(**MARGARET** *laughs.*)

Thank God I found Jesus.

MARGARET. Your mother loves Jesus –

TENDI. Oh please. I mean – sure. But Mom is very *religiously* Christian. I mean, a true spiritual connection? Where you are not just doing the liturgy perfectly with your stiff fellow upper-class congregants? I mean seriously, she probably couldn't quote one verse in the bible with a gun to her head.

(*Enter* **ANNE.**)

ANNE. Where's my tea?

TENDI. Finally! (*Rushing it to her.*) Right here Auntie!

ANNE. Serve me while I am sitting ah!

TENDI. Sorry!

MARGARET. Mahkwee-tey. Annie!

(**TENDI** *waits for her aunt to sit;* **ANNE** *takes a luxurious amount of time to do so. Finally,* **TENDI** *serves her the tea.*)

ANNE. Ah!

Right. Now. (*Finally.*) Where is he? (*Bellowing.*) YAY! MUKWASHA CHRIS!! MUKWASHA CHRISI!!

CHRIS. (*Running out of the study.*) Right here Auntie!

ANNE. Good. And we must sing at the ceremony.

TENDI. Who?

ANNE. Myself and Maggie. We must come in with the African brooms and sing – to usher you forth.

TENDI. Auntie, we have a very specific program; my pastor is "ushering" me forth – Dad walking me down the aisle – bridesmaids –

ANNE. That is things of the whites.
(*To* **CHRIS**, *with a smile.*) Not to offend!

TENDI. No, it's Christian too.

ANNE. Ya, ya we all love Jesus what, what, but your peoples Must be honored there. Your language must be heard there. We will sing.

TENDI. But –

ANNE. (*Sips her tea, cutting* **TENDI** *off.*) SO! Let me explain the process properly. (*Sips her tea.*)

TENDI. (*Aside to* **CHRIS**.) She Cannot be serious. We are already doing THIS for the African side!

CHRIS. (*Hushed.*) One battle at a time babe.

ANNE. (*Sips her tea.*) So, now, Mukwasha Chris, (*Sips her tea.*) to explain (*Sips her tea.*) this is Not how we would do roora if things had been prepared PROPERLY; (*Glaring at* **MAGGIE**.) if we were doing it right, it would be a big affair a *big* affair, the house full of people, singing, celebrating, I would NEVA be conducting, it would be an uncle or someone like that, I would just be one of the mothers, being honored. BUT it must be done. SO. I will conduct. (*Sips tea.*) And! I want this to be clear! The point of roora is to bless this union. Understand?

CHRIS. Yes Auntie.

TENDI. Yes Auntie, thank you.

ANNE. (*Smiles so brightly.*) You are welcome. SO. Firstly we will need the munyai.

CHRIS. Okay.

TENDI. What *is* that, Auntie Anne, in English please.

MARGARET. The munyai is the go-between, the groom's representative so to speak. He negotiates on behalf of the groom, preferably a relative.

CHRIS. I can't negotiate for myself?

ANNE. *(Laughing.)* Ah ha! Neva!

MARGARET. No. That would be...very taboo. You are not even supposed to be in the house.

CHRIS. Really?

TENDI. Wow.

MARGARET. Yes, you are called back in once the families have agreed on everything.

CHRIS. Okay. I'm not sure who I could get at this short a notice.

ANNE. Someone from your family.

CHRIS. What about my mom?

ANNE. Ha! Neva!

MARGARET. That would be...taboo.

TENDI. Oh my goodness.

CHRIS. Okay, okay. A relative...man...I guess, oh God. I guess Brad?

TENDI. Yeah, his younger brother. That works right?

ANNE. Very good. So that is the munyai.

CHRIS. *(Pulling out his phone.)* Oh man.

TENDI. Babe, we have no choice, and he's fine!

CHRIS. Yeah, well, he's a little *brash*,
    (To **ANNE.***)* he just came out of the military / I'm not sure how he'll –

TENDI. Babe!

CHRIS. Okay, I'll give him a call, I guess he'll have to do.

ANNE. *(To* **MARGARET.***)* Ane mombe here? [Do they have the cattle?]

MARGARET. Come on kani! You can't be serious Mai Carol!

ANNE. I am serious! I am very serious! It must be done!

TENDI. What? What now?

ANNE. We need –

MARGARET. NOTHING! Kids, go wait in the bedroom.

TENDI. What? Why?

ANNE. Ya, why?

MARGARET. It's a part of the proceedings.

TENDI. Please Aunties, we need to get this rolling!

MARGARET. The faster you go –

TENDI. Okay! Let's go.

>   (**CHRIS** *and* **TENDI** *exit.*)

MARGARET. WHERE do you expect this boy to get cows?

ANNE. He can get them!

MARGARET. From where? Makupenga here? [Are you nuts?]

ANNE. Aiwa mhani! Chinzwa! Ane marika! [No man! Listen! He has money!]

MARGARET. NO HE DOES NOT!

ANNE. SHHHH!!

MARGARET. She is the chief breadwinner! He works on human rights in Africa!

ANNE. *(Shocked.)* AH!

MARGARET. You want to drain this young man dry, you are crazy!

ANNE. Iwe, chinzwa kani [listen man], ane Mari [he has money]! He is a white!

MARGARET. ANNE! HAUNYARE! [HAVE YOU NO SHAME!] I am telling you he doesn't. His mother is a nurse. His father is out of the picture! This isn't Zim where every white has more money than every black!

ANNE. Kana! [No!] There is inheritance money ivo varungu vanowana [that these whites they can access].

MARGARET. Maiwee! Marvi was right. You are crazy. I agreed to help because I thought this was going to be SYMBOLIC! What are you going to do with a cow in America anyway, you want a plane ticket also for it to go back with you?

ANNE. They can buy them for us IN ZIM!

>   *(Beat.)*

MARGARET. How much?

ANNE. What?

MARGARET. How much are you looking for?

ANNE. You know how it works!

MARGARET. Okay, mombe yeumai –

ANNE. Ya, and the list.

(She hands **MARGARET** *the list.)*

MARGARET. *(Perusing the list in utter disbelief.)* Eeeey! ANNIE! Come on kani!

ANNE. Chi? [What?] That is VERY reasonable, very, very reasonable, you don't KNOW what people back home are asking for.

MARGARET. *(Reading out loud.)* A designer woman's suit, blue or red.

ANNE. Hmm hmm, those are my colors ka.

MARGARET. Designer shoes, black, open toe, with no more than a two and a half inch heel

ANNE. Hmmm hmmm, mavaricose veins ano netsa. [My varicose veins are a problem.]

(Brandishing the back of her shins.)

MARGARET. Two more woman's suits dash color and dash size?

ANNE. Those ones are for you guys ka. You fill in *ma* blanks.

MARGARET. Two pairs of shoes dash and dash.

ANNE. *Ma* blanks for you to fill futi [also].

MARGARET. A man's suit, shoes and Jasey?

ANNE. Ehe.

MARGARET. A coat?

ANNE. Ehe.

MARGARET. For Baba Tendi?

ANNE. Ehe!

MARGARET. And *good quality luggage*?

ANNE. Shuwa. Mine are finished.

MARGARET. ANNIE! THIS IS NOT A SHOPPING SPREE!

ANNE. SHHHH! Iwe kani! As if this is new to you!

MARGARET. *(Struggling to contain herself, continues reading aloud.)* Mombe yeumai [cow for the mother], a fatted heifer that has not given birth yet.

ANNE. Hmm hmm.

MARGARET. And a larger bull!

ANNE. Ya baba ka. [For the father.]

MARGARET. Goodness. Now what is this on the bottom?

ANNE. What?

MARGARET. THIS, this, number?

ANNE. Ah ah? Why are you confused? That is the vhura muromo [open the mouth], then that is the makatizisana ["you have left us"], then that is the rusambo [dowry] ka!

MARGARET. *(Counting.)* Four, three, three point five – TEN THOUSAND DOLLARS?!

ANNE. SHHHH! Iwe, nyarara kani [be quiet]. Yes, ten thousand dollars. This is standard ka! You should see how much they are charging back home.

MARGARET. Anne, we CANNOT do this wanzwa [do you hear]!

ANNE. That is our way!

MARGARET. It is NOT our way to bankrupt people!

ANNE. IWE! You know how this works! Back then it was chickens and goats, now it's this ka! What did you expect?

MARGARET. Nothing! It's just – it's just – We're in America –

ANNE. SO?

MARGARET. So they will see it…differently.

ANNE. And SO? Why do I care?

MARGARET. NO! Chinzwa ka. [Listen.] This is why Marvi was against it! 'Cause they will see it as…as… *(Hushed, saying it like it's a dirty word.)* materialism. Like we are grubby, greedy Africans, / like we –

ANNE. Who CARES Maggie. Honestly. Who? Not me. Not my ancestors. Let them think what they want! This is our way! These whites will produce it. Ucha wona [you shall see] baby sister.

(Collecting her notes and gathering herself.)

Come on, call them back, we are wasting time.

MARGARET. *(Switching tactics.)* So how much of this is for you?

ANNE. Ah, what do these ones need it for.

MARGARET. Which ones?

ANNE. Ehe, vana Marvi na Donald. They didn't even want it!

MARGARET. So it's for you?

ANNE. Didn't I ask for a suit for her and you and Donald?

MARGARET. SO you take the rest?

ANNE. Iwe, chinzwa [you, listen], there is Nothing back home. Nothing. This one wants to say she is the "executress of Baba's estate" showing off. When was the last time she checked on the electric bills or the septic tank? The place is in disarray! Then she wants to sit here like she is the Queen of America. We need that money ka. She doesn't. This money can excuse all that neglect she is doing. We haven't even been able to fix the toilets for *ma*lodgers! For a year! I tell her, I call, I send *ma* emails. She ignores. She says, "You live there, take care of it." As if it is somebody else's business. Take care of it! Does she even UNDERSTAND what it is like to be a retired nurse IN ZIM! My pension went to DUST the minute the Zim dollar fell. People like me, we cannot survive, a nurse for THIRTY-FIVE YEARS, not a penny to show for it. GONE to Gono [notorious Reserve Bank Governor of Zimbabwe]. "Take care of it." HOW?!

(Beat.)

So now, oura daughter is marrying, she is now providing where her mother was not. It is all family money ka. We are her mother also.

MARGARET. I know but –

ANNE. BUT WHAT? *(Suddenly enraged.)* You people want to sit in this country and act like Zimbabwe no longer exists? IT EXISTS!! And it is where YOU are from! You people haven't been back ONCE! As though there is some other land where you were birthed and suckled! You want to keep these whites happy, FOR WHAT? They are going to take *our* daughter to be in *their* family! She is going to lose her name, she is going to start having these makaradhi ["colored" mixed-race children] children that will talk like her, *(Imitating an American accent.)* "MAWM, I want to go to the MAWWL MAWM! I want PIZZA!" Will she even bring them home, even ONCE? Will they even know that their mother is a TSOKO! The daughter of an ancient peoples! That *her* mother once fought for her people's freedoms! They won't even HAVE a totem, let alone a language! They will be asked where they are from and they will say, MINESOOOTA, and that will be IT! Then imagine *their* children! They will probably marry a white futi [also] and the kids will look like whites! They'll be some sort of blue-eyed wonders! We will be gone! Wiped out! History! And they will know nothing about where they are truly from. We are losing Margie! We are losing our people, our children! Our blood! Our roots! Her whole life we let Marvi raise her like she was a white. A black American at Best. CLUELESS as to who she truly is! It is time Margie, it is time to bring her back. So that is why I was brought here. To be an equalizer! Tip *ma*scales [the scales]. Insist our ways are followed AND RESPECTED! And at the very least we can get their monies! After all, what else is the white good for?

   (A couple of beats pass.)

Now.

   *(**MARGARET**, silenced, gets up from the couch.)*

MARGARET. *(Suddenly.)* Okay, just…just wait, wait one second let me –

(A knock at the door.)

*(**TENDI** and **CHRIS** come out of the study.)*

CHRIS. Aunties I think that's my brother. He can be the munyami.

ANNE. MUNYA*Y*I! Ah!

CHRIS. Sorry! Munyayi.

ANNE. Okay. Good.

MARGARET. *(In a hushed whisper.)* Just, just let me be the MC, let me assist Chris' munyai, ndapota, please.

BRAD. Hey bro, *(Giving her a massive hug.)* Tendi.

TENDI. Ha! Wow! Hey Brad, thank you, so much for doing this –

ANNE. *(Beat.)* Okay. But you try to stray and I will take ova.

CHRIS. Hey Man! Thanks for making it over so fast, we need you.

MARGARET. Agreed.

ANNE. Now,

BRAD. Wow! *Need* me! Cool! No problem man. What's going on?

TENDI. *(Taking his coat.)* A lot. Don't worry, it should be quick and painless.

ANNE. Yay! Hurry UP!

CHRIS. Brad, just, be chill. Please.

BRAD. What? I just got here bro –

ANNE. Come in here Ka! Where is Nyasha? Tendi, go and get a blanket. Once you have found the blanket, go to the bedroom.

TENDI. A *blanket*?

ANNE. YES, a blanket. Didn't I already tell you? And stay there. Gotwe ari kupi? [Where is the youngest?] Where is Nyasha? Mukwasha [Son-in-law] Chris, who is this?

BRAD. Whoa. What did she call you?

CHRIS. Auntie Anne, Auntie Maggie, this is my younger brother, Brad. Brad, this is Auntie Anne and Auntie Maggie

BRAD. *(Stepping forward and bear-hugging them both.)* Hey, Aunties! I love that! It's a pleasure to meet you Auntie, Auntie.

MARGARET. Oh! Oh my! Well, yes and, and you.

ANNE. Ah Ah Ah! Chris, you must teach your family how to greet their elders *respectfully*.

BRAD. I'm, I'm sorry Ma'am I just thought, you know, we're family now!

ANNE. EVEN SO! And NOT YET! In our culture, when you greet an elder as a man, you do your arm like this *(Demonstrating on herself.)* and then once we have all been seated – *(She sits.)* Sit down.

>   *(They sit.)*

On the floor. For the proceedings, that is where you will sit. You have not proved worthy for our daughter YET, so you sit in a lower position.

BRAD. *What?*

CHRIS. Right, great, no prob Auntie.

>   *(He sits on the floor, pulling* **BRAD** *down with him.)*

ANNE. Good. Then you say, "Makadii MaiGuru" clapping your hands like so.

>   *(Clapping her hands in the manner specific to Shona men.)*

BRAD. Ahh...alright, alright, I'm game, ah, a Meku –

ANNE. Ah ah. MAKADII.

BRAD. Mekuday.

ANNE. Amaiguru.

BRAD. I am a guru?

ANNE. Then I say, "Ndiripo, makadii wo." Then you say, "Ndiripo."

BRAD. Iniripo.

ANNE. And you keep clapping your hands ka.

BRAD. *(Quickly resuming clapping.)* Alright, alright! No clicks?

ANNE. What?

CHRIS. *BRAD!*

BRAD. I'm just kidding! Nothing, Ma'am, ah, nothing!

ANNE. Okay, good. Mukwasha Chris! You must work on that with him hey!

CHRIS. Yes Auntie, absolutely.

ANNE. Good. So this is the munyai [negotiator/go-between]?

BRAD. / The what?

CHRIS. Yes. Will he do?

ANNE. He will do very nicely.

BRAD. *(To* **CHRIS.***)* I'm the *what*?

TENDI. *(From entryway.)* Auntie, I have the blanket.

ANNE. So get in the bedroom KA!

TENDI. *Okay. Dang.*

> *(She goes into the study and shuts the door.)*

ANNE. From now on Mukwasha Chris, you do not address us directly. You only speak to us through your munyayi. Understand?

CHRIS. Yes Auntie.

ANNE. Good. Maggie, go and get a bowl. These girls don't listen. A big one, wooden, weku isa sadza [to put sadza – traditional meal], not some small cereal thing.

> *(A beat passes,* **MARGARET** *doesn't move.)*

Now.

> *(***MARGARET** *reluctantly gets up and goes to the kitchen. She returns as quickly as she can and places the bowl on the coffee table.)*

Where is the father?

CHRIS. Donald?

ANNE. Yes.

CHRIS. I'm not sure.

ANNE. Ahh!

TENDI. *(From study.)* Aunties! We are seriously out of time! Please move with haste!

ANNE. IWE! GET BACK IN THERE! THERE IS NO SUCH THING AS HASTE WITH ROORA!

TENDI. Oh. My. God.

ANNE. Shut that door!

TENDI. OKAY!

> *(She shuts door.)*

ANNE. *(Looking at the two men like a lioness with her prey.)* Now. Let's get started.
We kutanga – Maggie!

MARGARET. *(Mortified, translating.)* To start with –

ANNE. Unofanirwa kutirakidza ruremekedzo –

MARGARET. *(Translating.)* You must...show your...respect to us by –

ANNE. Nekutanga basa nechipo....

MARGARET. *(Translating.)* Commencing the proceedings with an initial...gift.

> **(ANNE** *holds the wooden bowl out and points into it expectantly.)*

ANNE. In here.

CHRIS. Got it –

ANNE. Unotaurirwa ne munyai chete!

CHRIS. Sorry...sorry what?

MARGARET. She says you should only speak through your munyai, as she is speaking through me.

CHRIS. Got it.

BRAD. What the –

CHRIS. Shhhh.

ANNE. Maggie! *(Pointing at the bowl.)*

MARGARET. Oh gosh. Okay, so if you could both just place some *small* token to commence within the bowl, it is called vuramuromo. Meaning opening the mouth or commencing to speak, so to speak.

CHRIS. Cool. Ah...

> *(Opening his wallet, he pulls out some bills, nudging* **BRAD** *to do the same.)*

BRAD. Seriously?

CHRIS. YES!

> (**BRAD** *and* **CHRIS** *approach the bowl – bills in hand.*)

ANNE. Ah ah ah! Wombera ka!

CHRIS. Ah...

BRAD. Sorry what now?

MAGGIE. She wants you to approach the bowl clapping your hands as she showed you earlier and on your knees –

CHRIS. Oh, right, of course!

> (**CHRIS** *commences to clap his hands, head bowed; he shoves his brother.*)

BRAD. All Righty!

> (*They approach the bowl and place their bills in –* **ANNE** *looks and shakes her head.*)

ANNE. Ah! Hey! Shoma!

MAGGIE. Annie!

ANNE. IWE!

MAGGIE. She is saying...she is saying...that it –

ANNE. TOO LITTLE!

CHRIS. Oh! Okay! Ah...

> (*Pulls his wallet back out and shoves his brother to do the same.*)

BRAD. Come ON.

CHRIS. BRAD.

BRAD. *(To* **CHRIS***, in a hushed whisper.)* DUDE what is going ON?!

CHRIS. I'm not sure anymore. But chill, I'll get it back to you –

> (*They re-approach and place more bills in the bowl.* **ANNE** *takes a look, skeptically.*)

ANNE. *(After a long look.)* Ohright. Ngatitange.

MAGGIE. *(Visibly relieved, translating.)* Great. So let us start.

ANNE & MARGARET. Saka pakurooresa, tino fanira kuremekedza mwana wedu – [In light of this union, we must honor our daughter –]

(DONALD rushes into the room and sits.)

ANNE. Ah! Baba Tendi, wauya [you have come].

DONALD. Ya, just for – a bit.

ANNE. Okay, so where were we –

MARGARET. We must honor our daughter –

ANNE. Yes!

ANNE & MARGARET. Akabudirira! Igweta, munhu anokosha, hatingati ayende mahara kana nemari shoma, shoma, shoma. [She has excelled! She is a lawyer, a valuable gem, we cannot part with her cheaply, we cannot part with her cheaply, we cannot part with her cheaply.]

(DONALD nods almost undetectably.)

MARGARET. *(Through gritted teeth.)* They Get It.

ANNE. *(To MARGARET.)* Iwe! *(Back to her diatribe:)*

ANNE & MARGARET. Ne su Mashona, zvinhu zvinofanira kuitwa NEMAZVO. [With us, the Shona, is that, things Must be done PROPERLY.]

MARGARET. I think they get it!

CHRIS. Repeat this for me Brad –

BRAD. I still don't get this man, this is *nuts* –

CHRIS. *Just do it!*

BRAD. *Alright!*

CHRIS. We understand.

BRAD. We understand.

CHRIS. And respect these proceedings accordingly.

BRAD. And respect these proceedings accordingly.

CHRIS. We also believe we are receiving a gem.

BRAD. We also believe we are receiving a gem. Oh my God.

CHRIS. Shhh…

ANNE. Interpret Margie!

MARGARET. Oh my goodness –

(To **ANNE** *and* **DONALD**, *in Shona.)* Vari kuti vari kuziva kuti vari kuwana munhu akakosha. [They are saying they understand and respect our proceedings accordingly and believe they are receiving a gem.]

ANNE. Zvakanaka. [That is good.]

DONALD. Zvakanaka. [That is good.]

MARGARET. *(To* **CHRIS** *and* **BRAD**.*)* They say that is good.

ANNE. Now to start with.

> *(She reaches into her bra, pulls out her list, and puts on her reading glasses.)*

MARGARET. Oh God, Baba Tendi, help kani.

ANNE. Iwe!

DONALD. *(Getting up.)* I should get back.

MARGARET. Ahh, Baba Tendi...

DONALD. It's best. For the peace. Carry on...

> *(He exits.)*

ANNE. *(Back to Shona.)* Chekutanga tinoda mombe yakasvika. [To start with, we will need a healthy heifer.]

MARGARET. *(Struggling to translate.)* To start with, we will need a, we will need a –
(In Shona, to **ANNE**.*)* Hatikwanise / ndapota, ndapota kani! [We can't, we can't do this, please, let's just skip this, please!]

ANNE. *(Ignoring her, to* **BRAD**, *in English.)* Firstly, foremostly / we will be needing a –

> *(/ The front door slams.* **NYASHA** *stands in the entranceway, shivering in her pajamas.)*

MARGARET. Nana! What in the world!

NYASHA. *(Teeth chattering.)* I went for a walk.

ANNE. In your night dress?!

NYASHA. I needed tttttooo th th th think. Ddddiiid I mmiissss Rrrrrorrrra?

ANNE. No! Go to the study. And don't disturb – NOW, as I was saying –

NYASHA. I cccccaaan'ttt feeeeel mmmmyyyyy legggggsssss.

> (*She begins to hyperventilate and topples to the ground.*)

ANNE. Ahhhh iwe! *Ma*dramatics! Margaret!

> (*Rushing to* **NYASHA**'s *aid.*)

Anne kani! The girl is not well. Get a blanket!

BRAD. Ma'am, she is going to need to be human heated.

MARGARET. What?

BRAD. She is going to need to be heated by skin to skin contact. So you're going to have to –

MARGARET. Why? We are not out in the woods!

BRAD. She is in hypothermic shock, a blanket is not going to cut it –

MARGARET. TENDI! MARVI! (*Looking to her sister.*) ANNIE! DO SOMETHING!!

ANNE. What?! We don't have this back home! We are in the tropics! Tora gumbeze! [Get a blanket!]

> (**TENDI** *emerges from the study.*)

TENDI. What in the?

MARGARET. (*Fiercely attempting to warm* **NYASHA** *up.*) GO get blankets, a space heater.

> (**NYASHA** *starts to lose consciousness.*)

Oh my goodness! Nyasha! Nyasha!

BRAD. Auntie, you're gonna need to do skin to skin –

MARGARET. What? No – we can use a –

BRAD. Ma'am – she's passing out – anything else will be too much of a shock to her system.

MARGARET. But –

> (**BRAD** *rips off his shirt.*)

BRAD. Ma'am, ah Auntie, I'm sorry, I'm going to have to do this.

MARGARET. Do What?

BRAD. Auntie, please, step aside for a sec.

CHRIS. Auntie, let him do it, he was in the military, he knows what he's doing. You do know what you're doing, right Brad?

(*MARGARET reluctantly moves aside as* **BRAD** *takes* **NYASHA** *and rips off her pajama top.*)

ANNE. HA!! Ari kuitei? [What is he doing?] Ah ah ah!

(**BRAD** *holds* **NYASHA** *tightly to his chest, cradling her head.*)

(**TENDI** *rushes back in the room with a space heater; she plugs it in and points it at her sister.*)

(**MARVELOUS** *and* **DONALD** *finally enter and survey the scene. There is a prolonged silence.*)

(*Finally:*)

MARVELOUS. WHAT THE F–!

(*Lights out.*)

ACT TWO

Scene One

(The room is still. We see DONALD enter holding the map of the southern African nation. He hoists it back on the wall, squares it up carefully, stands back, and observes it for a long moment. Finally, he turns and walks out of the room.)

(NYASHA enters, bundled up in a robe, a woolly hat, and a blanket. BRAD enters from kitchen, fully dressed once again. He hands NYASHA a mug of a hot concoction.)

BRAD. From your aunt. Aunt Maggie.

NYASHA. Thanks.

> *(Beat.)*

You can stop staring at me that hard, we've already gone to second base and all. What is this?

BRAD. It's from Guatemala, naturally decaffeinated, your Aunt Maggie claims it heals all ills. Might check out one of her meetings next week.

> *(Beat.)*

NYASHA. *(Sipping the concoction.)* Ugggh!

> *(Pushing it away.)*

BRAD. You okay?

NYASHA. Yeah. Thanks.

BRAD. Thank *you*.

NYASHA. For *what*?

BRAD. Having your little incident.

NYASHA. Really?!

BRAD. Yeah, it let me be...useful.

NYASHA. Okaaay...well you're welcome, I guess.

BRAD. It's just up to then, I was looking like a real idiot in here. Didn't know WHAT was going on.

> *(Beat.)*

Chris has always been the golden child. Our family is mainly a bunch of hicks. So everyone was impressed and inspired by Chris. Chris graduated summa cum laude, Chris went to Africa, Chris is helping kids with malnutrition, Chris just visited the UN. Chris the hero. He certainly never needed me for anything. Till today. So, thank you.

NYASHA. Well, glad to have been of assistance. Aren't you like a decorated soldier or something?

BRAD. *Decorated?* No. I'm the screw-up who got someone pregnant at eighteen and had to go INTO the military to pay for child support.

NYASHA. Ah.

BRAD. Yeah. SO what about you?

NYASHA. Me?

BRAD. Well you obviously have *something* going on. Are you the family fuck-up too?

NYASHA. NO! Why would you say that?

BRAD. Hahaha Ha! Okay.

> *(Beat.)*

You're the youngest right?

NYASHA. What does that have to do with ANYTHING?

BRAD. So you are.

NYASHA. Listen GI Joe –

BRAD. Wow.

NYASHA. Just because we had a – a mortifying moment – and you got to be a real American Hero, doesn't mean you can start Dr. Phil-ing me – comprehende?

BRAD. Si.

  (Beat.)

NYASHA. I'm sorry. That was rude.

  (Beat.)

 She made me mad.

BRAD. Who?

NYASHA. Tendi.

BRAD. So you decided to get hypothermia on her wedding weekend to fix her?

NYASHA. NO!

  (Beat.)

 I needed to think.

BRAD. I get it. In subzero temperatures.

NYASHA. Exactly.

BRAD. I get it.

NYASHA. Good.

  (Beat.)

 I'm not crazy.

BRAD. Never said you were.

NYASHA. I don't know why I do some of the things I do though. It's just – my mother –

BRAD. Yeah, she seems intense.

NYASHA. Oh God. Oh GOD. And when I get around her, doesn't matter how much I have made progress in my life in New York, doesn't matter how many new mantras I have learnt. Or how close I have gotten to really figuring out who the hell I am. I get around her, I walk through THAT door, and I'm a kid again. *(Snaps her fingers.)* Just like that. I'm in ninth grade again arguing why I should be allowed to quit the fucking violin! Tendi's *just* like her. You'd think going to Africa would impress them.

  (She does a yoga mini "lion.")

BRAD. Well. I'm impressed.

    (Beat.)

NYASHA. *(Surprised at that.)* Huh...

    (Beat.)

BRAD. So.

NYASHA. So.

BRAD. I'm Brad.

NYASHA. Oh. Nyasha.

BRAD. Nice to meet you.

NYASHA. Yeah. And thank you by the way.

BRAD. Any time.

    (Beat.)

Does that have a meaning?

NYASHA. What, my name?

BRAD. Yeah.

NYASHA. Yes.

    (Beat.)

BRAD. *(Laughing.)* What does your name mean?

NYASHA. Grace.

BRAD. Beautiful.

NYASHA. What does BRAD mean?

BRAD. Ha! Probably average white guy.

NYASHA. Ha ha ha. Almost funny.

BRAD. Ouch. Almost. Well at least I got the pretty lady to smile at me.

    (Beat.)

NYASHA. Listen, you can't start hitting on the chick you just stripped naked and resuscitated. Too creepy.

BRAD. I know. It is, it really is and yet I can't seem to help myself.

NYASHA. How on earth can you find me attractive after that –

BRAD. It's very easy. You've already shown me your vulnerable damsel in distress side. So any tough stuff I know is just a mask. No guesswork. Very hot.

NYASHA. Oh Jesus.

BRAD. Hahahaha Ha.

(*Beat.*)

So what do you do?

NYASHA. I'm a singer-songwriter, and a feng shui consultant.

BRAD. Wow, a feng sh– I don't think I've ever met one of those.

NYASHA. Well that tells me you need one.

BRAD. Right. You're probably right. I do. Need one.

NYASHA. OMGEEE! Stop it already.

(*They stare at each other for a few beats.*)

Get a few drinks in me at the reception and maybe –

BRAD. My wish will be your desire?

NYASHA. Not all that, but hey, who knows. I mean, shit, you've already seen my tits.

(**BRAD** *laughs.*)

BRAD. And they were... /

NYASHA. AH!

BRAD. I'm sorry! But you are hot, you're very hot. That's just the truth.

NYASHA. Oh God. (*Blushing.*) Really?! Well, thanks, I guess.

BRAD. Thank *you*!

(*Beat.*)

So can *you* tell me what I'm doing here? There is some crazy shit happening in there!

NYASHA. Oh, it's a ceremony, traditional, that marries the bride and groom.

BRAD. And the groom *pays* for her??

NYASHA. No! He's showing his gratitude for her, to the family. Come on! It isn't that different in any culture. When a woman gets married she gives up her name, the kids she bears have his name, she is propelling his lineage, same thing here. This is acknowledgement of that. It shows that you value what you are receiving. Back in the day it was with goats and cows. Now it's – this.

BRAD. Huh. Well, I walked in here with money in my wallet and now I'm broke so it sure feels like he pays for her!

NYASHA. Stop. It couldn't have been that much!

BRAD. Not really, but I felt it was just getting started.

NYASHA. Nah. It's just to say we did it, you know. Are you the munyayi?

BRAD. Yeah, I guess I am.

NYASHA. That's very cool.

BRAD. Ha. Yeah, I guess it is.

> *(Beat.)*

Chris doesn't ask for, you know, anything from me. We were so close when we were kids but, now, he went all Jesus freak, we just speak different languages you know?

NYASHA. *Do* I. I think they are holding out till their wedding day! I really think Tendi might be a *virgin*!!

BRAD. Oh *dude*! Wow! Once again different / languages!

NYASHA. Languages!

DONALD. *(From study.)* Eh, Brad! Can you join me for a moment?

BRAD. Absolutely sir! Oh, one thought though, about your mom. How to deal with her, based on a little I know about moms.

NYASHA. What?

BRAD. Just make her happy.

NYASHA. Ha! That. My friend. Is impossible.

BRAD. You're her kid. It can't be.

(He jumps up, winks at **NYASHA**, *and exits.)*

*(***ANNE*** *enters, singing:)*

ANNE.
"TAUYA NAYE NEMAGUMBEZE, MOROORA! TAUYA NAYE!
TAUYA NAYE! MOROORA!" MUKWASHA CHRIS! YAY!!!
DZOKAI! DZOKAI! [COME BACK! COME BACK!] COME
ON! NGATITANGE! [LET'S START!] MAGGIE!

(Continues singing.)

MARVELOUS. NOW! Obviously I will have to be a part of
this since the moment I leave my house to *others'*
devices everything falls apart. So where were you with
it?

*(***MARGARET*** *rushes back in.)*

Get on with this, the child has a rehearsal dinner to
attend. And Nyasha, try to keep out of trouble for the
rest of your stay kiddo.

NYASHA. AH! Whatever man.

MARVELOUS. Ridiculous.

*(Seeing map, she grabs it off the wall and
stuffs it in the coat closet.)*

The man is losing it.

ANNE. RIGHT! So where were we then –

MARGARET. *(To* **MARVELOUS.***)* Please, control her!

MARVELOUS. Oh! Now you want me to!

MARGARET. Yes, please, I am sorry, I thought, I thought this
was right, I thought I could but she is on a rampage –

ANNE. Eyyyy, can we proceed?

MARVELOUS. Hmmm hmm. Go ahead.

MARGARET. What are you –

MARVELOUS. Shhh!

ANNE. Good. Now, we were at the point of Mombe Dza
Amai.

CHRIS. Right. And what is that again –

ANNE. Yay! You don't speak! That is what your munyai is for –

CHRIS. Right. Sorry.

ANNE. SHHHH!! He is the one we re-commence with. Where is he?

NYASHA. I think he is in the study with Dad.

ANNE. Ahhh! Tendi, go and get him.

NYASHA. I'm Nyasha by the way.

ANNE. Good, you know who you are. GO and get the munyai!

NYASHA. Alright! Geez!

(She exits.)

CHRIS. So –

ANNE. SHH!

CHRIS. I just –

ANNE. SHHH! No talking. Only through the munyai.

(BRAD enters, rushing to CHRIS' side.)

BRAD. Sorry everyone. Dude, your father-in-law is seriously cool. We are going to play squash tom–

ANNE. AH HA! You enter like this –

(She claps her hands in the manner appropriate for a Shona male.)

And say, "Tipindewo."

BRAD. Oh God, okay, Tipy deyo –

ANNE. Keep clapping!

BRAD. Okay, so – sorry Auntie.

ANNE. Then I say, "Pindayi." *Then* you sit. On the floor. And – *(She shakes the bowl at him.)* To recommence negotiations ka!

BRAD. Right – *(He digs in his pockets and pulls out a couple singles.)* Man. This is all I have left.

ANNE. Okay, we will do an IOU.

Now, to begin again, with – mombe yamai.

CHRIS. Ask on my behalf what a mombe yamai is – and stop hitting on my father-in-law.

BRAD. What?

CHRIS. / ASK!!

ANNIE. / ASK!!

BRAD. Uh, okay, wow. So, ah, on behalf of Chris, what is that then? *(Whispering ferociously.) He* asked *me* man –

CHRIS. / SHHH! Yeah right!

ANNE. It is – ah ah!

CHRIS. Not you Auntie!

ANNE. Don't talk!

CHRIS. Sorry!

BRAD. You always think I'm up / to some mess man.

CHRIS. SHHH. 'Cause you always are –

BRAD. I'm telling you – *he* –

ANNE. *(Clicks her tongue in annoyance.)* AH AH SILENCE! It is –

MARVELOUS. *(Who has been sitting quietly and composed throughout this whole exchange.)* It is a gift to the mother but it's fine, I forfeit it –

ANNE. Ah!

MARVELOUS. Let's move along shall we?

ANNE. Iwe Marvi, usatange, usatangekani. [Don't start, don't start.]

MARVELOUS. What? I am saying I acknowledge the gesture and am thankful for it, but I forfeit it – it's fine.

> *(Beat.)*

Oh and Donald wants to forfeit dzababa [for the father] also.

ANNE. AH!

MARVELOUS. So let us just get to the part where we sing and all that and have tea. I have some gourmet chocolate almond cookies! Come on Maggie, what is that song Amai loved / "Makanaka baba"!

ANNE. Marvi! We must do this properly kani!

MARVELOUS. We are the parents, the chief recipients, there is no rule in the Muzezuru Shona handbook of customs / that stipulates we cannot forfeit our right to gifts in receipt of our daughter!

ANNE. What handbook? Iwe! You know how it works –

MARVELOUS. And there is nothing that says I can't say I don't require the gift – Chris, my son, you can make myself and Donald a lovely dinner sometime.

ANNE. YOU –

MARVELOUS. You are a lovely young man to indulge our antiquated customs, we love you.

CHRIS. I – I love you too.

MARVELOUS. Even more for it, if that is even possible! But really, / it is the thought that counts after all – as –

ANNE. Marvi –

MARVELOUS. Her parents we are just pleased with your effort and respect.

ANNE. Marvi!

MARVELOUS. TENDI!! Come down, we are going to sing a song to honor your grandmother and have some tea!

    (**TENDI** *exits the study.*)

TENDI. Thank goodness! I've gotta GO!

ANNE. Tendi get back there!

TENDI. What's going on?

ANNE. We have Not completed this thing.

MARVELOUS. Yes we have! Your father and I have forfeited our gifts – but received and appreciated this lovely gesture – as the parents of the bride / we feel that is –

ANNE. You are not –

MARVELOUS. All that is needed, the beautiful gesture of acknowledging –

ANNE. You ARA NOT!

MARGARET. *(Turning ashen.)* Anne, PLEASE, NDAPOTA KANI!

MARVELOUS. *(Oblivious.)* Excuse me, Maggie! Let's sing the song, / how does it go again? You were good at that stuff –

ANNE. IWE! YOU ARA NOT THE MOTHER!

MARVELOUS. *(Stopping as though hit by an invisible freight train. Quick to recover –)* Well yes, in African culture we are all the mothers blah blah blah –

ANNE. NO! STOP IT! You are NOT the MOTHER OF THIS GIRL!

MARVELOUS. ANNE! DON'T YOU DARE!

MARGARET. Annie ndapota, ndapota kani ndapota ndapota / ndapota ndapota! [I beg of you!]

TENDI. What. The. Hell. Is going on right now?

MARVELOUS. NOTHING! Your aunt is just displaying her usual dramatics!

ANNE. *(Adamant and resolved.)* NO! I'm telling her now! *(To* **TENDI.***)* / This is not your mother. Your mother the woman who birthed you, was oura sista.

MARGARET. ANNIE!!

MARVELOUS. NO NO NO NO NO NO NO NO NO!! / Iwe Annie!! Uri Muroyi Iwe! MUROYI! [Annie you can't do this. You are a witch you, A WITCH!]

TENDI. WHAT?

ANNE. My sweet sister Florie. That was your mother. She is gone so, WE ARE NOW ALL YOUR MOTHERS! I, as the oldest, am actually the CHIEF mother here. Your mother would want you to HONOR your heritage. She fought for the freedoms of her peoples. Your mother died when you were a SMAALLL girl, a baby, and we decided that Marvelous would raise you as her own.

MARVELOUS. *(Suddenly vicious.)* WE DECIDED? WE DECIDED?! You came along and all you wanted were Florie's CLOTHES!! You weren't in the smallest BIT concerned with the welfare of this little baby girl!

ANNE. You must take pride in your customs and your culture, don't let ANYONE *(Looking pointedly at*

MARVELOUS.) take that from you. That's what your mother would have wanted.

MARVELOUS. SHUT UP ANNIE!

TENDI. *(Crumbling.)* Oh my God so Dad isn't my dad?!

MARVELOUS. Of course he will always be your dad and I AM your mother! I raised you, I changed your diapers, I took you to your first day of school. I am your mother – it doesn't matter –

TENDI. YES IT DOES!! I'm thirty-four years old! WHEN were you planning on telling me I have a whole different set of parents? A whole other family? WHEN?! I'm getting married for Christ's sake! WHEN?!

NYASHA. Oh my God Tendi –

MARVELOUS. We were going to tell you my darling girl, we were, it was just, you were happy and you are so close to your father, how could we –

TENDI. DON'T TOUCH ME!

> *(She gets up and exits the house, **CHRIS** seeing where she is going,)*

CHRIS. Babe, wait it's – freezing out there.

> *(He opens the closet and grabs a couple coats; the colorful map drops to the floor with a thud. He runs after **TENDI**, shutting the door behind him.)*

MARVELOUS. GET OUT OF MY HOUSE! I SHOULD NEVER HAVE LET YOU IN! GET OUT!!

ANNE. AH! It's what Florie would have wanted! You put this upon yourself!!

MARVELOUS. BULLSHIT!!

NYASHA. DAD!!

ANNE. She was nothing like you! NOTHING! She believed in the power of her OWN people! She died for that! Look at you! I should have kept her. I should never have let you bring her here!

MARVELOUS. Kept her to become WHAT?! A beggarly failure like *you*?!

BRAD. Okay, ah, Aunties! Let's all retreat to our corners for a second. Nyasha, take your mom upstairs.

(*Assuring* **NYASHA**.) I took a class in conflict resolution –

(**DONALD** *appears at the foot of the stairs.*)

DONALD. What is going on?

(**DONALD** *grabs* **MARVELOUS**' *hands.*)

MARVELOUS. She just told her Donald. She just told her.

(*They lead* **MARVELOUS** *out.*)

(*And for a few brief moments, the house is still.*)

ANNE. Ah, it had to be done, ka.

DONALD. My baby. My baby girl...

TENDI. Get the fuck out. I can't fucking breathe in this fucking house. Everyone get the fuck out.

MARGARET. Okay. Come on Annie.

TENDI. CHRIS COME HERE! I NEED YOU TO – / If you love me you'd –

CHRIS. Tendi! NO! This is nuts! What in the world does –? *If I loved you?!*

TENDI. I don't know! I don't know shit right now! All I know is – Oh GOD – I have gone thirty-four years keeping it together *literally* and for WHAT? Oh my GOD. I'M A LAWYER CHRIS!! AND I'M A MOTHERFUCKING OUTLAW! Oh my God! SO please, if you love me, just do it to me come here –

(*She tugs at his belt, which is already undone.*)

CHRIS. "Do it to you"?! Tendi! This is NUTS! THIS ISN'T YOU!

TENDI. WHO THE FUCK AM I CHRIS?! ALL of my life I have lived a FUCKING LIE! COME HERE!!

(*Following him around the room, he dodges her.*)

(*Catching him, pulling his pants down.*)

CHRIS. Tendi!

*(**MARVELOUS** coming down the stairs.)*

CHRIS. Tendi! Tendi!

TENDI. What the – GET BACK UP THERE!

MARVELOUS. Tendi – I...I –

TENDI. GET BACK! I NEED A MINUTE.

MARVELOUS. But –

TENDI. GET. BACK.

MARVELOUS. Okay, okay.

> *(She retreats, shutting the door behind her.)*

TENDI. AHHH! No. Come on Chris – now –

> *(She pulls her underwear off from under her skirt.)*

CHRIS. Honey! No! Stop! *(Sitting down.)* We have come so far. Just remember Jesus is in the midst of this storm.

TENDI. WHERE? WHERE?! He let those PEOPLE lie to me. OH GOD now I get it! Now I get why she was so FUCKING HARD ON ME!

CHRIS. Tendi! This isn't you! You don't *talk* like this –

TENDI. I never got it! Never understood why.

CHRIS. *(Getting up to console her.)* Tendi, she loves you, she –

TENDI. Oh, my God. Everyone always said I looked like her and not like Dad... *(She starts to crack.)* He's not my... who the hell is my... NO Fuck that. We are doing it now –

> *(She goes back to disrobing, hiking up her skirt.)*

CHRIS. TENDI! WHAT DOES THIS ACCOMPLISH?

TENDI. SHHH!

> *(She grabs for his now naked crotch, concealed by his shirt, and begins to caress it.)*

CHRIS. AHH! Ahh, Te– Tendi, Tendi ah...hhhhhaa...you, think this is what you want, but / I know you...ahh hahhhaaa... I know you and...and...

TENDI. Shhhh...wow...okay...wow...okay, okay...we are gonna do this... / Shut up, let's just do it baby, please, come on.

> *(She takes his hands and places them under her skirt.)*

CHRIS. TENDI...ahhhh... We...we can't...we...oh man... ahhhh...someone could...ahhhh...

> *(**BRAD** peeks out the door as if on military lookout – sees them, grins, nods, and shuts the door quietly, pulling **ANNE** back just as she tries to get by him.)*

(Pulling away.) NO! TENDIKAYI!! You are in shock, you are not thinking clearly and I will not take advantage of that.

TENDI. But –

CHRIS. OR be used as your de-stress dildo! *(Recovering.)* Oh God. *Man. (Tucks himself away, takes a few deep breaths.)* We – we made a decision! And it wasn't just your decision it was also MY decision to wait until we were joined as man and wife before GOD *and* man before we make love. And you can't make me break that vow to dislodge your hurt. You have to face this moment. You are a powerful, principled woman of God. THAT IS who you are. Whoever birthed you comes a far second to THAT identity. Don't let anything or anyone steal that from you. Be you.

TENDI. What? An Outlaw?

CHRIS. NO, YOU. *(He kisses her.)* You astounding, gorgeous, loving woman that I am ecstatic to have a ton of mind-blowing sex with for the rest of my days. Or at least for as long as you'll let me!

> *(**TENDI** laughs through tears and finally falls into his arms and weeps. Takes a deep breath and looks around, realizing for the first time the silence of her surroundings...)*

CHRIS. You are also... You are also an African woman.

TENDI. Wholololo.

CHRIS. And maybe, maybe today is the day.

TENDI. The day that what?

CHRIS. That you – that you face what that really means.

>   *(Beat.)*

TENDI. Can everyone proceed to the living room. NOW
please.

>   (**BRAD** *slowly opens the study door.*)

BRAD. That was quick! All done?!

TENDI. What? Yes.

BRAD. Life-changing right?

TENDI. What?

BRAD. It'll get better and better.

TENDI. Can you all proceed to the living room please!

>   *(Everyone trails downstairs,* **MARVELOUS**
>   *leading the way, her head held high and*
>   *dignified.)*

MARVELOUS. Of course my dear.

>   *(They all go and sit down,* **MARVELOUS**
>   *and* **ANNE** *in separate corners.* **BRAD** *stays*
>   *standing, on standby, eyeing both women*
>   *cautiously.)*

TENDI. Okay. SO. Tell it and tell it all. Who was my mother?

>   (**ANNE** *starts to speak and* **MARVELOUS**
>   *quickly interrupts her.*)

ANNE. It was –

MARVELOUS. AH! It was your Aunt Florence.

TENDI. Where was I born?

ANNE. In Rusape Marvelous. / In Clearwat– AHH!

TENDI. Woah woah woah. Rusape what? Rusape Minnesota?

ANNE. No. Rusape Rhodesia.

>   *(Beat.)*

You were born in Zimbabwe.

TENDI. / Are you kidding me?!

MARVELOUS. ANNIE! OH MY GOD SHUT IT IWE!

ANNE. Ah Why?!

TENDI. *(Forcing herself to take deep breaths.)* So wait...I am not an American citizen?

ANNE. No.

/ You are a TSOKO! A daughter of noble peoples!

MARVELOUS. IWE ANNIE! NYARARA! [BE QUIET!]

ANNE. What? Am I wrong?! She must KNOW! And your mother was a hero!

MARVELOUS. BULLSHIT!

ANNE. Ah! Haunyare? [Have you no shame?]

TENDI. WHAT? SO how the HELL have I – have I –? How have I gotten student loans and lived and worked and – This doesn't make any SENSE!

DONALD. Well...

MARVELOUS. DONALD!

DONALD. It's enough. Let the child know who she is.

> (**TENDI** *looks weak on her feet,* **CHRIS** *holds her up, looking deeply into her eyes, as if willing her.)*

TENDI. Dad – what? Is this why you had me invite Auntie? WHAT?

MARVELOUS. *Had her what?*

TENDI. He put me in touch with her – and said I should bring her here for roora.

> *(Beat.)*

MARVELOUS. You must be joking.

TENDI. Dad. I need you to speak right now.

MARVELOUS. Yes. You better!

DONALD. I didn't – I hadn't planned this through to this end. But...yes...Marvi, I felt...we couldn't allow her to... to –

MARVELOUS. TO What?

DONALD. To get married and not connect to her culture, who she really is. Where we are from, there is no marriage without roora. We did it! Something borrowed, something blue, *what is that*?

MARVELOUS. Ha.

     (Beat.)

So this is where we are now Donald?

TENDI. / Who am I Dad? Tell me? *Please, just, tell me.*

DONALD. Okay, okay, let, let me try. Well – We went to Zim in 1979, / with our daughter –

MARVELOUS. Baba Tendi DONT!

DONALD. Do you suggest, at this point – we withhold this?

     (Beat.)

We went with our daughter – our daughter Tendikayi.

NYASHA. Whaaa...?

MARVELOUS. / No...

     (She turns her back to everyone, barely able to hear it recounted.)

DONALD. She was eighteen months old. You were two years old. When we got there, Tendi, ah...your mother Florie...she was a, very involved with ZANLA, the armed forces that were fighting the colonial regime. She was a revolutionary really. Very, very brave. / Very brave.

MARVELOUS. Oh please –

ANNE. Ah AH! She was!

     (To **TENDI.***)* She died valiantly / my dear –

MARVELOUS. Don't you dare! Don't you dare!

ANNE. It was the colonial army, / those demons, they came –

MARVELOUS. She *took* my child into a BATTLEFIELD!

ANNE. NO SHE DID NOT!! / They were ambushed, they were ambushed!!

MARVELOUS. She took my child, my baby girl on some *mission*?!! SHE was RECKLESS –

MARGARET. *(Weeping.)* / Oh please, please, please...

ANNE. KANA!

MARVELOUS. SELFISH! ONLY THINKING OF her barbaric *chimurenga* [struggle] and NOTHING ELSE.

ANNE. She was A HERO! A BRAVE DAUGHTER OF THE SOIL! / Something you could NEVER BE!

MARVELOUS. A HERO?! AT WHAT COST ANNIE?!! AT WHAT COST TO *ME*?!

MARGARET. *(With a force we never imagined she had.)* STOP! STOP!! STOP!!!

> *(Beat.)*

> *(Collecting herself. Goes over to* **TENDI**.*)*

The child – is right here. Please.

> *(Beat.)*

Tendi, your mother and father – ah – Donald and Marvelous, they went back to Zimbabwe with, with Tendi – they were moving back for good actually. It seemed independence was imminent. There was a day that your mother was with – the...the other Tendi, and – all we know is that they went to a village – there was a possible leak that she was there, to the colonial authorities and all we know is there was a skirmish of some sort and they were...they were shot.

NYASHA. That's so horrible. You always said she died in a car crash Mom.

TENDI. Where was I?

MARGARET. You were visiting your grandmother.

TENDI. And where was my father?

MARGARET. He – he had died in the struggle a few years prior. On the field. Very active in the struggle. Very revered. We'll never really know...

TENDI. So how did I –

DONALD. We were not going to just leave you there.

TENDI. So you gave me my dead cousin's identity?!

MARGARET. It was assumed that it was you with her. We just...we just decided not to dispute it. It's what your mother would have wanted – to have you go to Marvi...

ANNE. HUH!

MARGARET. Please, Annie!

NYASHA. *(Processing.)* So there was another Tendi and this Tendi isn't Tendi?

MARGARET. Not now Nyasha.

(Beat.)

TENDI. My name...what was it?

MARGARET. Petulance

TENDI. Pet– Petulance?!

MARGARET. I would ask her, don't you mean Prudence? Petunia? Perpetua even. She would say, "NO! Petulance."

MARVELOUS. Your mother was never very...cultured.

ANNE. Why? It is a lovely name ka! A name of resistance! Just because she didn't go to MIP'S or whateva!

MARVELOUS. It's MI*T* for the Forty Thousandth time!

ANNE. "Not very cultured"! Haunyare? [Have you no shame?] Aren't you fearful of how you've been speaking of the dead like that!

> *(Beats of silence ensue around a family shell-shocked and pulsating with the pain of old wounds never healed.* **TENDI** *sits next to her fiancé, who feels powerless to console her, as does everyone else in the room.* **CHRIS** *finally looks up at his brother, not sure where else to turn for help. Finally:)*

BRAD. Beg your pardon. Just to jump in the mix a bit here, as the munyayayie. In light of what has been revealed, the real question is: Where do we go from here? What is done can't be undone, but there is a wedding. That's one way you can, you know, work past this. You guys, are, you are strong. You are. And you love each other. A lot. You've been in a real war zone and you left no man behind, you're the real deal man. And this won't, it won't break you. Makes you stronger if anything. Truth man. It's a beast.

> *(Beat.)*

But, I digress. Or not! Quick FYI, there is ah, a ah rehearsal dinner, in approximately sixty-seven minutes, so...

MARGARET. Who is this guy?

CHRIS. Marry me.

TENDI. Oh God, I don't even think I can –

CHRIS. No. Baby, look at me. You do what you were always going to do. You marry me. Aunt Annie, what is the brideprice, just hit me with it –

MARVELOUS. AH!

ANNE. Ah, he is a good one. He is a *good* one! Here is the number, I'll amend it some because, ahh, there are damages.

TENDI. DAMAGES! WHAT like I'm damaged goods?!

ANNE. Not, not exactly, but ahh, there have been lots of deceits.

MARVELOUS. You are a beast.

ANNE. What? I am amending ka! If he still wants her after all this, ahh, he is a good one.

> *(She pulls her paper list out of her bra, grabs a pen, and rewrites a number.)*
>
> *(Hands it to CHRIS.)*

CHRIS. Okay. *(He takes a deep breath and opens it.)* Oh. Okay. That's workable. Do you need it all today?

ANNE. Oh no, just a down payment then ma installments are fine. MoneyGram.

CHRIS. Great. No prob. I can handle this.

TENDI. Chris! HOLD ON! I don't even know if I can do this anymore –

I just, I just have to ask this – would you guys have taken me, even have wanted me, if the real me hadn't passed?

DONALD. Of course we would have, you were already a daughter to us.

MARVELOUS. *(Almost inaudibly, trembling.)* I should never have trusted her with her – we should *never* have gone back.

TENDI. Is this why Mom? Is this why you were so freaking hard on me?

MARVELOUS. Ha.

> *(Beat.)*

You can hate me Tendi, for my lies, for how hard you say I was on you, but I was determined, you WERE NOT going to be your mother. That was not going to be *your* story. NOT on my watch. And now...look at you. Look at you. You are accomplished, you are beautiful, you picked well, and you are STRONG. STRONG.

> *(Beat.)*

MARGARET. She did do a lot, your mother – Marvelous – for you, to make sure you had a good life.

MARVELOUS. Maybe not enough.

ANNE. She was a *good* woman. A *warrior*. And you look just...just like her.

TENDI. I gotta...

> **(DONALD** *reaches for her in an attempt to console her; she pulls away sharply.)*

Tell her the rest. Tell her why. No more secrets.

> *(She sits, her gaze intent on her father.)*

MARVELOUS. Oh! There is more! Delightful. Tell us what?

> *(Beat.)*

DONALD. Ahhhk.

MARVELOUS. Tell us what Donald?!

DONALD. I want to go back.

(Beat.)

MARVELOUS. WHAT?

DONALD. I want to go back.

MARVELOUS. Ah?

DONALD. I have to go back and contribute something before –

MARVELOUS. Before *what*?

DONALD. Marvi! We sit in our Midwestern living room watching American political pundits rant and we ignore our own plights?! This isn't our *home / Marvi*.

MARVELOUS. IT IS –

DONALD. NO! NO IT IS NOT!

(Beat.)

Ahhhk.

(Beat.)

Emmanuel called, a while back, and he said something, that I just, I just haven't been able to shake. I was referencing some news article about the *issues* and the *suffering* and he...he yelled at me really. My own baby brother. Told me I had no right to talk about suffering I chose to never experience. That I fled from. That I had no right to call it suffering. It wasn't mine to name. He, he told me I was a refugee. Of my own making. An *American African*. Marvi, I just can't, I can't have that on my tombstone. Look at how we raised them Marvi. With Halloween and softball practice but not one Shona word in their mouth? It's shameful.

(Beat.)

I know... I know how much home hurts for you, the pain we felt there; that's why I couldn't... I didn't know how to...how to...

(A few beats pass.)

The last time...the last time I saw her...she...she wrapped her little arms around my neck. She looked at me like, like I was her hero. I kissed her right here – *(He points at his forehead.)* Then I let her go with Florie. And I have let her down EVERY DAY SINCE. I left, never to return, and what does that make me Marvi? I am worse than any despot, any oppressive regime! I'm the one who abandoned ship! Who left my own people to drown and smothered their cries with western convenience and customized La-Z-Boys. I didn't just drop the ball, I kicked it off the fucking cliff! It's sickening. It's bloody sickening. And it's empty Marvi! It's so empty in here right now. *(Pointing at his heart.)* I've got to go Marvi. I don't know what that even looks like, but I have accepted it. Finally.

(*Beat.*)

Finally.

(*Several beats of silence.*)

MARVELOUS. How long – have you been trying to tell me for?

DONALD. A few months.

MARVELOUS. *Really?*

DONALD. Yes. The map...

MARVELOUS. *That* was really supposed to let me know?

DONALD. No, no, but Marvi! We invested in that place, we raised funds, we sent back books and clothes, brought attention to the struggle in local press. We were *in it*. And we were ALIVE, we were so alive then Marvi. Then we punished that whole place, we – I found it in the garage and...I wanted, I just wanted to remind you of that time, when we used to boldly proclaim where we were from –

(*Beat.*)

MARVELOUS. It's a sinking ship DONALD!

(*Beat.*)

You couldn't get out of bed Donald. When she... You couldn't get out of bed.

I carried you Donald. I carried you on my back. All of you. *This* is where we agreed to. Now you want to be an *African* again?

You can't just –

(Beat.)

We drove all the way to Penn State for the big game right after we got naturalized. To celebrate. 1986. Remember? You and me, snow blizzard and all, but we made it. And we roared as we embraced our fellow Americans. And we looked at each other in the eye and it was clear to me – our decision was so clear Donald. This was it. *Here.* I don't care WHAT they think of me back there. I didn't create that mess. I TOOK CARE OF YOU. That was my home. YOU Ha.

I guess I'm not home enough for you.

(Beat.)

So this is what I get.

(Beat.)

I won't go back Donald. I won't. I won't go watch you chase ghosts of yesterday. That place is finished.

(Beat.)

I'm here Donald. I'm standing *right here.*

(Beat.)

DONALD. Okay.

MARVELOUS. Okay.

(Several beats pass.)

MARGARET. Marvi. Forgive me, please, I just have to say this. Baba Tendi. Going back home. Offering your gifts to the people. That actually sounds amazing to me.

ANNE. Eh ey, it does.

MARGARET. Sometimes...you feel this thing right here. *(Pointing at her heart.)*

(Beat.)

MARGARET. It hurts. It hurts the soul.

ANNE. What, are you thinking about coming home?

(Beat.)

MARGARET. I wanted to – to be like you Marvi. Huh. Let's just admit it – it didn't work! It didn't fucking work. But I'm here now, got my green card! Living the dream! Huh. And the boys...shit.

ANNE. The boys are grown-up now.

DONALD. But you can *still* do it Maggie. Look at what you have accomplished here. You can be like Wangari Maathai, even like Ellen Sirleaf Johnson.

MARGARET. Oh please. Please. Please.

(Beat.)

But maybe, maybe I should have taken them home, Tongi at least. Once even. Maybe they'd be, they'd be – ahhhk. *(Picks up wine glass.)* What's the time check now, sergeant? Twenty-seven minutes and counting?

BRAD. We're down to forty-two minutes.

MARGARET. Tendi, are we going to this dinner, or what?

*(By this time, **TENDI** has walked over to **CHRIS**, who was on the other side of the room, trying to give her space. She looks deep into his eyes for a long beat.)*

TENDI. Okay.

(To everyone.) Let's try to make it there on time.

(Pause.)

Mom you okay?

MARVELOUS. I am fine.

*(**TENDI** hugs **MARVELOUS**. **MARVELOUS** then exits upstairs.)*

TENDI. Dad?

(Beat.)

You good?

DONALD. Just to hear you call me Dad. I am great. I'm going to put my proud daddy suit on.

> *(They embrace.)*

BRAD. Chris, you have to take me back to change.

CHRIS. Alright, let's get going then.

BRAD. I'll see *you* in a bit.

> *(He discreetly takes* **NYASHA***'s hand and squeezes it.)*

CHRIS. *(Under his breath.)* Brad, I will kill you bro –

BRAD. What?

CHRIS. You know what. That's my baby sister.

BRAD. Baby sister *cousin.*

CHRIS. I will – Don't even think / about it –

BRAD. / Dude, it's done –

CHRIS. *You'll* be done if you even *try* –

> *(***BRAD*** exits.)*

TENDI. Babe?

CHRIS. Yeah!

> *(***TENDI*** approaches him and kisses him.)*

TENDI. You are so amazing to me. You amaze me. That's the one thing I know for sure right now. I'll see you there?

CHRIS. Yes you will.

> *(***CHRIS*** exits. ***TENDI*** pulls out her phone; she tries to will herself to get back to it but just ends up plopping on the couch.)*

> *(***MARGARET*** goes to ***TENDI***, wraps her arm around her shoulder. ***TENDI*** buries her head in her aunt's shoulder. Exhausted. ***NYASHA*** goes to make an attempt to comfort her "sister" but stops herself, unable to quite make contact.)*

NYASHA. *(Shifting gears.)* What was the deal with the blanket Auntie?

ANNE. She was to be wrapped and presented like a gift –

NYASHA. Like gift-wrapped?

ANNE. Ahh...sort of...sort of...

MARVELOUS. *(From the stairs.)* Annie! Mai Carol!

ANNE. Yay?

MARVELOUS. Come up here so I can give you something decent to wear!

ANNE. *(Exiting.)* AH? There is *nothing* wrong with what I am wearing! Ah! You want me to dress like what? Eh? The Queen of England?

> (**MARGARET** *goes into the kitchen to refresh her wine. She returns to* **TENDI**'s *side.* **NYASHA** *pulls out her mbira case and unzips it. She starts to sing a tune – it is beautiful and melodic, a fusion of African percussiveness and a soulful ballad.)*

TENDI. Nyash – when are you going to get read–

NYASHA.

NDINI, NDINI, NDINE THE FEELING ITS IMI, IMIMI, ITS IMIMI, TIRI, KUZIVA/WA KUTI ITS NOW, NOW'S THE MOMENT FOREVER BEGINS WITH IMI, IMIMI, FOREVER BEGINS WITH IMIMI. YOU SEEM SOO, YOU SEEM SO VERY, SO VERY, VERY FAMILIAR.

> (She jumps suddenly, noticing her mother standing silently behind her.)

TENDI. You wrote that?

NYASHA. Yeah, well, I kinda just came up with it in the last day.

MARVELOUS. *(Holding a dress.)* Really?!

NYASHA. Yes Mother, really.

MARVELOUS. It, it's beautiful.

TENDI. Yeah, it is.

NYASHA. ...Thank...you...

MARVELOUS. Ya. You learnt a lot in Zim eh? Even the mbira!

NYASHA. Yeah. That was the point.

MARVELOUS. That's...that's impressive.

NYASHA. Thanks.

> *(A few beats pass.)*

What is that?

MARVELOUS. What?

NYASHA. That dress in your hand?

MARVELOUS. Oh this, *(She quickly puts it behind her back.)* nothing. Get ready, we don't want to be late!

> **(MARGARET**, *smiling broadly, exits upstairs.)*

TENDI. Yeah.

> *(Beat.)*

You wanna sing with Auntie Anne and Auntie Maggie at the ceremony? Maybe do that one tonight at the rehearsal dinner?

NYASHA. Uh, sure.

TENDI. Great.

> *(She gets up and returns to her phone, walking down the hall.)*

> **(MARVELOUS** *starts to exit.)*

NYASHA. Mom?

MARVELOUS. Yes?

NYASHA. *(Beat.)* I'm so sorry.

> *(Beat.)*

MARVELOUS. What is the song called?

NYASHA. Familiar.

> *(Beat.)*

I think.

MARVELOUS. Familiar. I like it. I like it a lot.

NYASHA. Thanks Mom.

MARVELOUS. You are welcome my dear.

> *(Beat.)*

Familiar. Keep playing. Please.

NYASHA. Ah...okay.

(**NYASHA** *goes back to playing the song, the plunky melodic chimes of the mbira filling the home.* **DONALD** *appears at the entrance, dressed and deeply moved by the sound. He enters the living room, approaches his wife, who is seated on the couch, and after staring at her for a long beat, asks for her hand. She stares back and takes it, raising to her feet. He begins to dance with her, moving to the music as though his soul is receiving long-deprived nourishment. She slowly begins to move to the music too, their movements manifesting their Shona roots as they sway to the ancient traditional instrument. As their daughter sings and plays they dance and dance in complete rhythm and harmony...together.)*

End of Play

9 780573 705694